Praise for *Kiss Me Like a Stranger*

"The title came from Gilda Radner, his third wife, and one of the many friends, lovers, and colleagues about whom he writes with striking candor. . . ."

—*The New York Times*

"Wilder tells plenty of entertaining stories about his work with everyone, including Jerome Robbins, Mike Nichols, Mel Brooks, and Zero Mostel . . . [it's] a reflective and well-written meditation on the life of someone who has more on his mind than the next big part or belly laugh."

—*Los Angeles Times*

"I always knew Gene Wilder was a remarkable person, but I didn't realize how remarkable until I read this brave, riveting book."

—Charles Grodin

"It's not an autobiography in the usual sense of the word. . . . It's an honest, affecting look at his life."

—*Kirkus Reviews*

"Gene Wilder is not just a uniquely talented and lovable performer, he's a gifted memoirist with a story to tell and a writerly commitment to emotional truth. The real delight lies in the prose—tight, funny, and fast as the breeze—and the insights about accident and fate that lodge in your mind long after the smile has left your lips."

—Letty Cottin Pogrebin, author of *Three Daughters*

"A wonderful addition to the entertainment memoir Gene pool."

—*Library Journal*

"A book to cherish. Here is the real Gene . . . irrepressibly funny, wise, warmhearted, and honest. In sharing with us the most intimate details of his extraordinary life on-screen and off, Gene shows all of us how to embrace the unexpected, pursue our passion, and seize joy every day. Give this book to someone you want to kiss."

—Pat Collins, film critic

gene wilder

kiss me like a stranger

MY SEARCH FOR LOVE AND ART

ST. MARTIN'S GRIFFIN ✺ NEW YORK

www.stmartins.com

Book design by Jonathan Bennett

Photographs on pages 73, 79, 119, 157, and 171 courtesy of Photofest. All other photographs and memorabilia are from the collection of Gene Wilder. Photograph on page 163 © Steve Schapiro.

"After a While," pages 218 and 219, courtesy of Veronica A. Shoffstall.

Library of Congress Cataloging-in-Publication Data

Wilder, Gene, 1935–
    Kiss me like a stranger : my search for love and art / Gene Wilder.
        p. cm.
    ISBN 0-312-33706-X (hc)
    ISBN 0-312-33707-8 (pbk)
    EAN 978-0-312-33707-0
    1. Wilder, Gene, 1935– 2. Motion picture actors and actresses—United States—Biography. I. Title.

PN2287.W45888A3 2005
791.4302'8'092—dc22
[B]

                                                            2004058475

10 9 8 7 6 5

contents

To Karen,
without whom I would be
floating like a cork in the ocean

kiss me like a stranger

Suppose you're walking out of the Plaza Hotel in New York City on a warm spring day. You breathe in the lovely fresh air as you step outside and walk down the red-carpeted stairs, saying a quick, "Hi, again!" to the uniformed doorman.

You want to go directly across the street to Bergdorf's Men's Shop on Fifth Avenue, but the Plaza fountain is directly in your path, with people from all walks of life sitting on the ledge of the fountain, eating sandwiches in what's left of their lunch hour, talking to their friends from the office, maybe flirting with some new acquaintance and whispering arrangements for a love tryst that night. Perhaps some are taking a short sunbath on this first beautiful day of the year or even sneaking in a quick snooze as they lean their backs against the famous fountain where Zelda Fitzgerald once jumped in fully clothed.

You can get to the shop on Fifth Avenue by walking around the fountain on the path to your left, or by taking the path to your right. I believe that whichever choice you make *could* change your life. I'm sure everyone has had these mysterious brushes with irony, perhaps referring to them years later as "almost fate." Here are a few of mine.

chapter 1

FIRST MOVEMENT

1962—New York

I walked into Marjorie Wallis's small office on West Seventy-ninth Street. I was very nervous.

"What do I call you?" I asked.

"What do you want to call me?"

"I heard Dr. Steiner call you Margie on the telephone . . . is that all right?"

"Margie it is! Sit down."

She indicated the plain couch in front of me. There were no pictures on the walls. Margie sat in a comfortable-looking arm-chair, with an ottoman—which she wasn't using—resting in front of her. Her face wasn't warm, but it wasn't stern, either.

"What seems to be the trouble?" she asked.

I couldn't bring myself to look at her.

"I want to give all my money away."

"How much do you have?"

". . . I owe three hundred dollars."

She looked at me silently for four or five seconds.

"I see. Well, let's get to work, and maybe by the time you have some money you'll be wise enough to know what to do with it. In the meantime tell me about . . ."

And then she asked me a lot of questions. "Your mother was how old? . . . How did you feel when the doctor said that? . . . Have you ever tried to blah, blah, blah?" I took so many long pauses before I answered each question that I thought she might throw me out, but she just sat there, with her feet up on the ottoman now, and waited. When I did start talking again, she made little notes on a small pad that rested on her lap.

What I couldn't understand was this: why on earth was I thinking about a fifteen-year-old girl named Seema Clark during all my long pauses in between Margie's questions? Seema kept popping into my head while I was talking about my mother and doctors and heart attacks and my Russian father and masturbation.

I thought Seema was Eurasian when I met her the first time— she certainly didn't look Jewish—but when we both came out of the synagogue together I realized that she must be Jewish. She was the most beautiful girl I had ever seen. I was only fifteen, but I had seen a lot of movies and I thought she looked like a very thin, teenage Rita Hayworth. I was her date when Seema had her fifteenth birthday party. There were eight or ten other kids at her house that night, all laughing their heads off at some wisenheimer who was "hypnotizing" one of the girls. I thought he was pretty stupid, but I enjoyed watching the cocky little faker who thought he knew how to hypnotize people because he'd read his uncle's book on hypnosis.

Seema held my hand while we watched the "hypnotist" go

through his fake talk. I knew she really liked me. She looked so pretty that night, with a pink barrette in her hair and wearing a brand-new yellow angora sweater. Her mother served all of us birthday cake and some delicious coffee. When all the other kids had gone home, Mrs. Clark showed me the coffee can, because I had said how good the coffee tasted—it was A&P's Eight O'clock Coffee—and then her mother said good night and left Seema and me alone.

We sat on the couch in an almost-dark living room and started kissing. I was shy, but I didn't want Seema to know how shy I really was, so I put on an act as if I were used to all this kissing in the dark with no one around. I thought that she was probably more experienced than I was and I decided that it was about time for me to feel a girl's breast. Well, I can't say, "I decided"—I was just going on what I'd heard from all the other boys my age, especially my cousin Buddy, who was nine months older than me.

It took me about eight minutes to get my hand near the start of Seema's breast—the hairs of her new angora sweater kept coming off in my fingers, which certainly didn't help any. After another three or four minutes, I finally put my hand on about one-third of her breast. As soon as I did, she jerked away. My mouth went dry. She looked at me with such disappointment in her eyes and said, "You're just like all the other boys, aren't you?" I flushed so hot I thought I'd burst. I couldn't understand why she didn't say anything during all the kissing and creeping up the fake angora. Why didn't she just say, "No," or, "I don't want you to do that," or anything but what she did say? I wanted to tell her that I wasn't at all like all the other boys, that I thought she would like what I was doing, that I thought she was waiting for me to do it. But I was too embarrassed to say any of those things. I just said, "I'm sorry, Seema," and then wished her happy birthday and got out of there as fast as I could.

Of course, this all happened in little pictures that popped into my head during the long pauses with Margie. The whole memory probably lasted only a few seconds. Margie's voice suddenly burst in:

"Where are you?"

". . . What do you mean?"

"Lie down on the couch. You're not as innocent as you pretend and Dr. Steiner assures me that you're no dummy. I want you to start talking and tell me everything that crosses your mind—*everything*—however embarrassing or insignificant *you* think it is. I don't know whether or not I can help you and I don't know how many times you and I will be seeing each other in the future, but whether it's one more time or several years . . . don't ever lie to me."

chapter 2

CAN A FEW WORDS CHANGE YOUR LIFE?

Milwaukee

I used to be Jerry Silberman. When I was eight years old, my mother had her first heart attack. After my father brought her home from the hospital, her fat heart specialist came to see how she was doing. He visited with her for about ten minutes, and then, on his way out of the house, he grabbed my right arm, leaned his sweaty face against my cheek, and whispered in my ear,

"Don't ever argue with your mother—you might kill her."

I didn't know what to make of that, except that I could kill my mother if I got angry with her. The other thing he said was:

"Try to make her laugh."

So I tried. It was the first time I ever consciously tried to make someone laugh. I did Jewish accents and German accents and Danny Kaye songs that I learned from his first album, and I did make my mother laugh. Every once in awhile, if I was a little too successful, she'd run to the bathroom, squealing, "Oh, Jerry, now look what you've made me do!"

* * *

Some people—when they step into the ring—lead with their left; some lead with their right. I always led with my sister.

It was a Saturday night. I was eleven. My sister, Corinne, was sixteen and she was giving an acting recital at the Wisconsin College of Music, where her teacher, Herman Gottlieb, had his studio. It was a small auditorium stuffed with about two hundred people. While everyone sat and waited for the show to start, there was so much loud talking that I wondered how Corinne would stand it. When the lights started to fade, everyone talked louder for a few seconds. Then they all whispered. Then . . . darkness!

A spotlight hit the center of the stage, and there was Corinne, wearing a full-length aqua gown. For the next twenty minutes she performed "The Necklace," a short story by Guy de Maupassant that she had memorized. All eyes were on Corinne. The audience was listening to every word. You could hear a pin drop. Everyone applauded her at the end. I remember thinking that this must be as close to actually *being* God as you could get.

I went up to Mr. Gottlieb and asked if I could study acting with him.

"How old are you?" he asked.

"Eleven."

"Wait till you're thirteen. If you still want to study acting, I'll take you on."

When my mother was in pain, the fat heart specialist came to our house. I say "fat" only because Dr. Rosenthal died of a heart attack a few years later, and even though I was very young, I instinctively associated his death with how many Cokes he drank whenever he came to our house. One day he came because my mother felt a terrible pressure in her chest. Dr. Rosenthal told me to go around the corner, where they were putting up a new house, steal a heavy brick, and then wrap the brick in a washcloth and place it on top of my mother's chest, over her heart. It sounded crazy. I waited until all the workers had left the new house, at the end of the day, and then I picked up a good-sized brick, tucked it under my sweater, and walked home as fast as I could. I wrapped the brick in a washcloth and placed it on top of my mother's chest.

"Oh, honey, that feels so good."

In the months that followed I would substitute my head for the brick. I'd push my head down with both hands as hard as I could, and she liked that even more than the brick.

One Sunday afternoon my dad dropped me off at the Uptown movie theater, so I could see a Sunday matinée. I didn't tell him that I'd taken his flashlight out of the utility closet and hidden it in my jacket.

After I paid the cashier and bought my popcorn and Milk Duds, I went into the theater, which was almost full. The picture had already started, but in those days most people were used to coming in after a movie started—they would stay until they saw a familiar scene in the next showing and then leave. This Sunday the movie was *Double Indemnity,* with Barbara Stanwyck and Fred MacMurray. It was in black and white.

I watched for about twenty minutes, but when it started getting mushy (kissing), I took the flashlight out of my jacket and began shining it onto the screen. When people looked around to see which punk was doing this, I shut the flashlight off, fast. When the audience settled down again, I switched the flashlight back on. I started making circles on the screen—my beam of light competing with the beam from the projector. I got such a feeling of joy from doing this, until the manager came down the aisle with a horrible look on his face and told me to come with him. I followed him into his office.

"What's your name?"

"Jerry Silberman. Please don't tell my father."

"Give me the flashlight."

He took my father's flashlight and kicked me out of the theater. It was drizzling outside. I felt ashamed, standing under the overhang in front of the theater, wondering whether or not to tell my dad about his flashlight and about the manager kicking me out. I decided it would be safer if I waited till my dad noticed the missing flashlight himself . . . and that might not happen for months. He was born in Russia but came to Milwaukee with his family when he was eleven. He wasn't dumb, but he was very innocent, and I knew what I could get by with if I wanted to evade a situation.

After I waited in the rain for an hour and ten minutes, my father drove up. I jumped into the car.

"So—how was the movie?" he asked.

"It was great, Daddy. It was really good."

I started taking acting lessons with Herman Gottlieb the day after my thirteenth birthday.

* * *

I was eleven when I learned about sex—from my cousin Buddy, naturally. We were both in a co-ed summer camp. I couldn't believe what he was saying.

"Oh, Buddy, what're you talking about?"

"It's the truth! You put your poopy into her thing—honest to God."

"Well, how could that ever make babies?"

"Because you've got to put your germs into her germs. That's how you do it."

". . . Well, what if you're embarrassed? I'm not going to take it out in front of a girl."

"Are you telling me you wouldn't like to show it to her if she showed you her whatcha-call-it?"

". . . Well . . ."

Then Cousin Buddy told this crazy idea to Alan Pinkus, another one of our friends. Alan was more shocked than I was.

"You're nuts."

"Well, how do *you* think you get babies, Alan? Do you think the stork brings them?"

Buddy tried his best to make Alan feel like a baby. Alan was embarrassed.

"No, of course not. . . . I just thought it came from . . . putting your saliva in with her saliva."

"You mean spitting at each other?" Buddy laughed so hard that I started laughing too. That was when I figured that Buddy must be right. He was an expert about these kinds of things.

We never talked about sex in my family when I was growing up. The only time I came close to asking about it was when I was in second grade and I was walking home from school with two other boys. We saw a naked lady through her living room window, lying on a sofa, scratching her tush while she read a book. When she saw three little boys staring at her, she jumped up and closed the curtains. We ran away, and I heard one of the boys use the word "fuck." When I got home, I didn't tell my mother about the naked lady, but I did ask her what "fuck" meant.

"You want to know what "fuck" means?" she asked, as she pulled me into the bathroom and turned on the faucet. She ran a bar of Ivory Soap under the water and stuck it in my mouth. "There! Now you know what fuck means."

I started crying, and then, as was her habit until she died, she started crying and begging me to forgive her. Begging and begging, until I finally went into her arms and she hugged me and kissed my tears and kept repeating, "I'm sorry, honey. I was wrong. Can you ever forgive me?"

My mother had a distant cousin who lived in Los Angeles and whose thirteen-year-old son was going to a place called Black/Foxe Military Institute, run by retired colonel Black and retired colonel Foxe. My mother's cousin said she thought it was a wonderful place, and it was in Hollywood, California. What she didn't mention was that her son was going to Black/Foxe as a day student, so he went home each afternoon after school.

Since my mother was ill and felt that she and my father couldn't give me the kind of training that I needed, now that I was thirteen—she thought I still didn't know how babies were made, and I didn't have the guts to tell her that I did—she got it into her head that Black/Foxe Military Institute might be the perfect answer. I think she was influenced by a movie called Diplomatic Courier, starring Tyrone Power. She thought that if I went to Black/Foxe, I would not only learn how to dance, play bridge and play the piano, but also how to be at ease with girls and learn everything there is to know about sex. So off I went to Hollywood. What else my mother didn't know was that almost every boy who lived at Black/Foxe came from a broken home—mostly they were sons of parents who wanted to get rid of their kids.

On my first night at Black/Foxe, I was assigned to a room on the second floor of the dormitory. When I walked in I was greeted by a short, tough-looking boy with acne all over his face.

"Hi, I'm Jonesy," he said. "We're going to be roommates for a long time so I'm taking this bed and you take that one."

When I got into my brand-new pajamas that first night, Jonesy started smiling at me and said, "Lemme corn-hole ya." I didn't have a clue what he was talking about. Then he told me to just lie down on my bed, facedown. He got on top of me and put his penis between my thighs and started pumping away until he had an orgasm. His "jizz" went onto my new pajamas, not into me. After he saw how upset I was, he never tried to do that again. He just jerked off in the closet.

This was 1946. When word got out that I was Jewish, some of the bigger boys started coming into my room and pounding me on the chest and on my arms. They didn't hit me in the face, and I was glad of that, but I couldn't understand why they wanted to beat me up. They never said why. One tall jerk named Macintosh barged into my room one day and started dancing around me—like an Indian in the movies, circling a covered wagon—and he kept singing, "We want the country! We want the country!" It scared me, but he didn't hit me, so I was okay. I remembered seeing some movie about initiation tests when you got into a fraternity, so I figured it was some kind of tradition to beat up the newest cadets. Then I found out that I was the only Jewish boy at Black/Foxe, so I finally understood the reason. But it still didn't make any sense.

I went to the sergeant's room at the end of the hall. He was a real sergeant who took the job at Black/Foxe when he retired from the army. I told him about all the beatings and asked him what I should do.

"You want them to stop beating you up?"

"Yes, sir."

"The next time one of them comes into your room, pick up a chair and smash it over his head."

". . . But . . . I can't do that. What if I killed him?"

"You asked me what to do. I told you."

I never went to him for help again.

There were several Mexican boys at Black/Foxe who came from very wealthy families. In those days bubble gum was very hard to come by, but the Mexican boys always seemed to have some. Instead of charging the other boys one penny—which was the market price for one of those pink bubble gum squares—they would charge one dollar. The tallest Mexican boy kept trying to sell me bubble gum, and I kept telling him that I didn't have that kind of extra money. Then he would say, "I give you a bubble gum if you jerk me off." I would laugh and pretend that he was making a joke, but I knew he wasn't joking.

On Fridays we always had a dress parade, which meant tie, jacket, hat, and well-shined shoes. We marched on the Black/Foxe drill field, which bordered on Melrose Avenue and Wilcox. People in the neighborhood would stand along the sidewalk each Friday afternoon to watch all the cute young cadets go through their routines.

As we were marching, one flamboyant, very likable young boy named Ronnie, who had a shock of bright red hair, kept telling me that he was going to be a big star one day. I would say that I was studying acting with Herman Gottlieb, who was a great teacher in Milwaukee. Ronnie would just answer, "You'll never make it, Silberman. I'll bet you anything you want that I'll be famous before you are." People who live in Hollywood are different from other people.

On Thursday afternoons I went to my piano lesson. The teacher was a nice-enough man but not a very good teacher. He assigned me just one song, called, ironically, "Nobody Knows the Troubles I've Seen." I don't remember if I ever told him about the troubles I was having with the other boys; I don't think so. And I know he wasn't that good a teacher to have purposely assigned that song to me as a way of using my unhappiness to help me play it better.

I wrote to my father and told him about all of this stuff, but he never showed any of those letters to my mother, I suppose for the same reason that I didn't write to her about it. At Thanksgiving I called my father and asked if I could come home for Christmas vacation. He said yes. When it came time to leave—for some reason I can't explain—I needed to say good-bye to Jonesy. My bags were packed, and the bus was waiting downstairs, but I searched all over the second floor for him. When I finally found him, he shook my hand and said, "So long, pal." Jonesy and I were never friends, and he was a jerk, but he never beat me up, and he had acne. I don't know why I needed to say good-bye to him. I'm sure it wasn't because he corn-holed me. I do remember that on one occasion he shared a box of candy with me that his aunt had sent him. Maybe it was because someone told him that chocolate wasn't good for acne.

My father and Corinne picked me up at the airport in Chicago, and we drove back to Milwaukee. I had on my blue, sort of itchy dress uniform, but I wanted to be wearing it when I walked into the house and saw my mother again.

She was waiting in our living room. When I walked in, she hugged and kissed me. Then she asked me to play something for her on the piano. Oh, God. I didn't think it would come that soon. I wanted to put it off. I made up some kind of flimsy excuse about not having practiced for several weeks, but she wanted to hear me play "just a little bit." So I sat down at the piano and played "Nobody Knows the Troubles I've Seen," and I played it terribly, with a hundred mistakes. She got up and went into her bedroom. I began to cry. My dad said maybe I should change my clothes and get ready for dinner. I took off my shirt and went into her bedroom to explain how I only had one lesson a week and how little time there was for me to practice, when she suddenly gasped. She was staring at my body. There were black-and-blue bruises on my chest and arms. My dad finally told her some of the troubles I had described in my letters. She started crying and begging me to forgive her, until I finally went into her arms and she kissed my tears and kept repeating, "I'm sorry, honey. Please forgive me. I was wrong. Can you ever forgive me?"

I never went back to Black/Foxe.

*　*　*

When I was fifteen, I went to a downtown movie theater to see *Great Expectations,* but before the movie started, they showed a short subject called:

VINCENT VAN GOGH

I had no idea who Vincent van Gogh was—I'd never even heard of him. Twenty-three of his oil paintings flooded the screen, one after the other, in full color. I don't know why they call it "dumbfounded"—I think they should call it "dumblosted," because after seeing the paintings, I was lost. When I walked out of the movie theater I started thinking about my second-grade teacher, Miss Bernard, who used to put up paintings from almost all of the other boys and girls in my class on the classroom walls—paintings that she considered worthy—but she never put up one of mine. She never told me why or gave me an encouraging word, but I got the message: "You're no good at art, Jerry."

The following Saturday I took an early train to Chicago to see the van Gogh Exhibit at the Chicago Art Institute. I could only stay for an hour because I had tickets for the two o'clock matinée to see Judith Anderson in *Medea.* My critical judgment wasn't fine-tuned yet; I thought the play was just okay. Then I walked to a theater about a half a mile away to see the five o'clock showing of Laurence Olivier's film version of *Hamlet*. That was okay, too. *Hamlet* let out at 8:10 P.M. so I ran—as fast as I could eat my hot dog— to see the 8:30 P.M. stage performance of *A Streetcar Named Desire*, starring Uta Hagen and Anthony Quinn. *That* was more than okay.

I think what I did was dumb—crowding all those great things into one day—but Milwaukee was a big "small town" in those days, and it would never have had a van Gogh exhibit or *Medea* or *A Streetcar Named Desire* with Uta Hagen. Today perhaps, but not in 1948.

My mother had wanted to be a pianist before she got married. When I told her about the van Gogh exhibit and how much I loved him, she gave me a little money to buy some paints. I took the bus to an art supply shop downtown and bought eight tubes of oil paint and two frames of stretched canvas, 18 × 24 inches apiece. The owner of the store helped me pick out a couple of brushes and advised me to take a small bottle of linseed oil. I also bought a print of a van Gogh painting for $3.50. It was called *Lady in a Cornfield*. When I got home, I set up shop in our basement, mounted the van Gogh print on a chair, and painted *Lady in a Cornfield*. My mother liked it so much that she had it framed and hung it on our living room wall, next to her piano. I've been painting ever since. So you didn't win, Miss Bernard. You didn't win.

MY FIRST PLAY

When I was still fifteen, I auditioned for the Milwaukee Players, which was a very good community theater that put on big productions of classics and also gave lessons in makeup. I passed my audition, and the first play I acted in—in front of a paying audience—was *Romeo and Juliet*. I played Balthasar, Romeo's manservant, and I had only two lines, but I also had a fencing scene, which I loved. It wasn't real fencing, of course; it was just sort of "try to make it look real" fencing.

My next part was the Messenger in *Much Ado About Nothing*. One evening, while we were in production, I got to the theater early and had just started putting on my makeup when one of the male dancers came in, very bouncy and cheerful. He had always been very friendly, but when he saw that we were alone, he started behaving strangely. I had never met a homosexual before—I had only heard Corinne talk about what were then called fairies—but this handsome dancer, who must have been at least ten years older than I was—started chasing me around the children's classroom that we used as a makeup room. I dodged in and out of the rows of little desks, trying my best to make the dancer believe that I believed that he was just playing a game. Just as I was getting frightened, two other actors came in, said, "Hi," and started putting on their makeup. I sat down at my desk and started putting on makeup again. I didn't look at the dancer until he knelt down next to me.

"You know I was just joking around, don't you?" he whispered.

"Of course! Are you kidding?"

I wish I had acted in *Much Ado About Nothing* as well as I did for the dancer.

chapter 3

"TAKE ME."

When Corinne was twenty, she went to act at the Reginald Goode Summer Theater near Poughkeepsie, New York. You had to pay ninety dollars a week for food and lodgings. In return, you got the privilege of acting with the famous sixty-eight-year-old Australian actor, Reginald Goode, in front of a real summer stock audience, six nights a week.

A call came to our home in Milwaukee. Mr. Goode suddenly discovered that he was one man short for his acting company. (I assume that some guy didn't want to pay the ninety dollars.) Corinne told Mr. Goode that her brother was an actor, and he told her to get me to Poughkeepsie immediately. I had just turned sixteen.

I was thrilled, of course, but my father wasn't—unless they waived the ninety-dollars-a-week fee they charged for the privilege of acting with Mr. Goode. After a lot of bluster, Mr. Goode agreed. I was on the train the next day.

The playhouse was a beautiful old barn converted into a theater. It held about five or six hundred people. All of the actors, except me, slept and ate in Reginald Goode's private house, across the huge lawn that separated the house from the theater. I was assigned to a unique bedroom inside the theater, just off stage left. The bedroom was about as big as a walk-in closet.

When I went to bed that first night, it was a little frightening. It was so dark when I shut off the one lightbulb and there were strange sounds all through the night. The old wooden barn was dancing with the wind. As I lay in bed, trying to fall asleep, I saw a name carved into the wall beside me, just above my head: "K T Stevens." I knew that name; I had read about her. She was a famous actress from fifteen or twenty years ago, and she must have slept in this same bedroom, probably in this same bed, and carved her name into the wall next to me, so that years later other actors would remember her. I ran my fingers over her carved name and whispered, "Good night, K. T.," then turned off my lightbulb and fell asleep.

The first play I acted in at the playhouse was *The Late Christopher Bean,* by Sidney Howard. I think I got more laughs than Mr. Goode had expected. When the two of us were alone onstage and the audience started laughing at something I did or said, he would lean down and whisper, "Wait for it. . . . Wait for it."

The play was so successful that he held it over for another week (or else he *had* to hold it over because he didn't have the next show ready, which was probably more likely).

The next play was *The Cat and the Canary.* Henry Hull had played the lead on Broadway; Bob Hope played it in the movie. Now I was playing the same part, but no one told me that "old" Mr.

Goode was married to this gorgeous twenty-three-year-old red-haired actress who was going to play my romantic interest. Her name was Rita. She explained to me, privately, that when we had our kissing scene, it shouldn't be a "real" kiss—which might throw both of us off—it should just *look* like a real kiss, by putting our lips on the side of the other person's mouth, just close enough so that it looked real. I thought, *Well—that must be how real actors do it.*

Mr. Goode worked in a bizarre way. After the evening performances we all made sandwiches from a big roast ham that was set out each evening on the kitchen table. We drank milk or soda (no alcohol), and then we rehearsed most of the night, until just before the sun came up. That's the way Mr. Goode wanted it. I loved it. For me it was very romantic. For Rita, too. Forget that "on the side of the mouth" business—by the fourth day of rehearsal, she started kissing for real.

Remember Seema Clark? The young Rita Hayworth with the fake angora sweater, who made me feel like a disgrace to God and my mother for trying to touch about half an inch of her breast? Because of her I still hadn't tried to touch a girl's breast. Kiss a lot, yes, but breasts were too dangerous. Of course, if Seema Clark had liked what I was doing and made some lovely sounds of encouragement . . . who knows?

We rehearsed *The Cat and the Canary* for five nights, and then, on the sixth night, before dress rehearsal and after strong signals from Rita, she and I drifted off towards the riverbank. We knew there would be a long break while they were changing the sets, so we lay down on the grass, near a little brook, and kissed and kissed. No breasts. No penis. While we were lying there, she said,

"Take me!"
"Take you where?" I answered.

I knew very well what she meant—I wasn't that dumb—but I wasn't prepared for the big time yet. I think that if Rita had been more aggressive on that particular night, my life would have taken a very different path. But she was careful where she touched me.

Later, after rehearsing till 5:00 A.M., I had just gotten into bed when I heard a knock at my door.

"It's me," Rita whispered.

I opened the door, and there she was, in her nightgown, looking as beautiful as a fantasy. She got into bed with me, and we started kissing. After about four minutes she said, "What do you think would happen if I touched you . . . here?" pointing to the bulge underneath my pajamas. Before I could answer, we both heard Reginald Goode calling out from somewhere on the lawn, near my bedroom door.

"Rita . . ."

He wasn't hollering, and he wasn't whispering. It sounded more like a father calling out to his daughter who had stayed out too late one night, but now it was time for her to come home. I felt that he didn't know for sure if she was actually with me but that he assumed she was. Rita got under the covers and wiggled down towards the bottom of the bed, so that if Mr. Goode did burst in, he wouldn't see her. I was scared to death. I do mean death—I imagined a shotgun.

"Rita?" he called again.

But he didn't knock on my door, which I was terrified he was going to do. He listened for another minute or ninety seconds. While I held my breath, I could hear him breathing—he was that close. And then he walked away. After three or four minutes Rita jumped out of bed, took a quick peek outside, and then ran across the lawn to the big house, just as the sun was coming up. Mr. Goode never brought up this incident to me.

Margie interrupted. (She rarely did, but we were now in our second year together, and I was used to it.)

"Now wait a minute, Mister Wilder. . . ." (She started using that little twist on Mister to emphasize whatever comic irony she was about to "epiphanize" me with.)

". . . Did you fondle her breasts?"

"No."

"Did she ever suck you?"

"No."

"Did you ever fuck her?"

"No."

"Did you want to?"

"Yes."

"Why didn't you?"

"I don't have a reason that makes sense."

"Then give me a reason that *doesn't* make sense."

". . . I thought it was wrong. I don't mean for anyone else, just me. I think I might have enjoyed it too much."

"Why would it be wrong if you enjoyed it too much?"

I lay motionless for almost a minute, searching for the answer, but I didn't know the answer.

Margie wrote something in her pad.

NO TIME FOR COMEDY

When the season at the Reginald Goode Theater ended, Corinne and I went to New York and saw *Death of a Salesman*, starring Lee J. Cobb and Mildred Dunnock. I couldn't believe what I was seeing. Even after I had started studying acting with Mr. Gottlieb, I didn't know that acting could be this real—it was as if what I was watching was actually happening. Until that night I had thought often about being a comedian, mostly because I had seen Danny Kaye in *Up in Arms* and then Jerry Lewis on television and then—for me, the king of them all—Sid Caesar, on *Your Show of Shows.* But after seeing *Death of a Salesman,* I had no more thoughts of being a comedian—I wanted to be an actor; perhaps a comic actor, but an actor, not a comedian.

I went back to Milwaukee and made a one-hour adaptation of *Death of a Salesman.* I played Lee J. Cobb's part, of course—a sixteen-year-old Willy Loman—and, along with two of my acting friends from school, we performed at churches and women's clubs all over Milwaukee and then in front of two thousand students at my high school. I also began reading *An Actor Prepares,* by Constantine Stanislavsky.

One afternoon, while we were performing at some women's club, I came to the scene where Willy Loman is trying to plant seeds in his backyard at night. I was very relaxed. I don't think there was any tension in my body or my mind. There was no actual earth, of course, only a wooden floor, but when I started planting . . .

ME (AS WILLY LOMAN): Carrots . . . quarter inch apart . . .

Suddenly I was in a backyard, not an auditorium, planting seeds. I knew I wasn't crazy. I heard everything that I was saying and what the other actors were saying. I knew I was acting in a play . . . but I also knew that I wasn't acting.

school years. It was reputed to have one of the five best theater departments in the country. I drove from Milwaukee to visit Corinne in Iowa City several times. We'd go to a football game together, and then I'd see her in one of the university productions. When I was seventeen, I saw her play the part of Gwendolyn in *The Importance of Being Earnest*. After the show I met her stage director, whom I liked very much. He looked at me for a second and then said, "When are *we* gonna get this fella?"

Corinne was invited to a party that someone was giving after the show. She told the host that she would like to bring her kid brother along. We walked into an old Victorian house, stuffed with college students. There were all kinds of things to eat and drink. Corinne introduced me to her roommate, Mary Jo, who had the most original lips I had ever seen—except perhaps for those of the French actress Jeanne Moreau, whom I had seen in a movie called *The Lovers*. She and Jeanne Moreau must have traded lip secrets. I wished that Mary Jo was going to my high school so that I could date her, but since she was a college student and I was what my father would have called "a high-school pisher," I honestly didn't think she would give me the time of day after we were introduced. I wasn't particularly handsome, and I certainly wasn't very experienced—especially when it came to the opposite sex—but, to my surprise, Mary Jo stayed with me during the whole party.

We sat down on a small sofa and ate hors d'oeuvres and watched everyone else in the room either kissing or drinking beer, or both. I don't know if I kissed Mary Jo first or if she kissed me—maybe it was both at the same time—but we started kissing. And we kept on kissing. I don't remember anything we said to each other—I just remember the kissing and the look in her eyes, where a small beam of light was reflected from a street lamp. When the party broke up, we said good-bye.

I slept in my used car that night and drove back to Milwaukee the next morning. The memory of Mary Jo's eyes stayed in my dreams for a long time.

———

As a high-school graduation present, my mother and father let me go to New York to see plays, provided I stayed at an inexpensive hotel. The old Taft Hotel on Fiftieth and Sixth Avenue fit the bill. I saw *Gentlemen Prefer Blondes,* starring Carol Channing. During her performance I was particularly curious how she could keep using her throat to make the guttural sounds she used, in her talking and singing, without going hoarse. After the show I stood at the stage door with a few other people, waiting for her to come out. When she did, she signed some autographs and then came up to me, expecting me to give her a program to sign. I don't know where I got the nerve to say it: "Miss Channing—does it hurt your throat when you talk and sing in that special way that you do?"

She looked at me as if I were some kind of country bumpkin and said, "I don't know what you're talking about." She gave me an autograph. I thanked her, and she left.

One evening, instead of seeing a play, I went to the Paris movie theater and saw Charlie Chaplin in *City Lights.* More than any other movie I've ever seen, *City Lights* made the biggest impression on me as an actor. It was funny, then sad, then both at the same time.

That fall I went straight off to the University of Iowa, acting in the first production of the year, *The Winslow Boy,* directed by Corinne's director, whom I liked so much and who had said, "When are *we* gonna get this fella?"

chapter 4

THE "DEMON" ARRIVES.

I suppose that everyone has had to wrestle with a demon at some time in their life. My Demon came out of hiding on the first day of spring, during my freshman year. It came out without warning, like a sudden eclipse of the sun—not in the disguise of alcohol abuse or drugs or gambling or sexual perversion—nothing like that. My Demon came out in the form of a horrible compulsion to pray. I say "horrible" because I didn't want to pray—I *had* to pray, wherever I was, even though I didn't know what I was supposed to be praying for.

When the compulsion came upon me, I would pray in front of whichever building I was about to enter for my next class. I would speak to God, out loud, but I tried to move my lips as little as possible when people passed by because I was afraid they'd think I was another one of those poor souls who hadn't bathed or changed clothes for a week, who usually smelled of urine as they mumbled up and down busy streets, talking to God, or the Devil, oblivious of everyone around them. I was excruciatingly aware of everyone around me, but I thought that if I were truly humble, then the presence of all these passersby shouldn't bother me. I kept on mumbling softly, trying to find out—as I prayed—what terrible thing I could possibly have done for which I needed God's forgiveness.

The craziness reached a point where, one morning, I plastered down my curly hair with Vaseline, just to prove how truly humble I was. When I looked in the mirror, I saw a freak. I was so embarrassed I didn't know how I could leave the house and go to class . . . but I did. I walked into my theater history class and sat next to my lunch pal, Betty Kanzell. She used to make fun of me if I missed breakfast and she heard my stomach gurgling, but on this morning she just kept staring at me.

BETTY: What the hell did you do to your hair?
ME: I'm just trying something. I'll tell you later.
BETTY: It looks horrible! Why did you do that?
ME: I told you—I'm just trying something. I'll tell you later.

And then one day—just like that, as if a motor or an electric switch had been turned off—the compulsion stopped. The Demon was gone. I felt as if I had just finished running in a long race, exhausted but exhilarated, and could now be a normal person again.

But three or four days later the Demon returned. The pattern repeated itself so often that I felt as Dr. Jekyll must have felt when he could no longer control the comings and goings of Mr. Hyde. I never knew how long each episode would last. Three days? A week? Two weeks? I never knew what set off the compulsion. The only small clue I had was wondering, every once in awhile, why I should have the right to possess money—if I should ever acquire any—when there were people all over the world who were dying of starvation.

Being on stage was the thing that saved me from myself. When I was in a play, I was safe. I did four plays in a row that first year, and then, for the fifth production, I was cast as Willy Loman's son, Biff, in *Death of a Salesman* . . . the play that had changed my life when I was sixteen years old.

On opening night the auditorium was packed. We had rehearsed for four weeks, and now I was lying in my "upstairs bedroom"—onstage—waiting for the cue for my first entrance. I didn't want to pray. "Not tonight, dear God, please!" Maybe the Demon forced his way in because it was this particular play. As I waited for my cue, I kept thinking that I could shut him out in plenty of time . . . but I couldn't; the fear of not praying overpowered me, even though it was a matter of seconds before my entrance. I saw both the play and my brain falling apart. Then, somehow, the obligation to the audience and Arthur Miller and my memory of Lee J. Cobb and Mildred Dunnock became more important to me than God. I heard my cue, said my first line . . . and I was safe for the remainder of the play. Years after that, I still carried the inexplicable conviction that once I stepped onto the stage, they couldn't get me (whoever the hell "they" were) and that I was safe . . . so long as the curtain was up.

I drove home for the Easter break. My mother was so happy to see me that I thought she'd burst. She was thrilled that I was going to be home for ten whole days. She laughed so much at my silly jokes that she peed in her pants again. "Now look what you've made me do, Jerry."

After dinner I found her in the living room, sitting on the couch and weeping quietly. I sat beside her. "What, Mama? What's the matter?" She said, "In nine more days you'll be gone."

A little later, at about seven o'clock, I said I was going to take a short walk around the neighborhood. It was still light outside, and I wanted to get some fresh air. After walking several blocks—with the Demon pounding at my consciousness, trying to get in—I found myself at an open field on the outskirts of town—a field I used to play in only a few years before. The Demon knew where he was leading me. I knelt down on the hard earth and started praying.

We were never a particularly religious family when I was growing up, in the sense of prayers at home or rituals, other than going to my grandparents for a meal on Passover and going to the synagogue on the high holidays. Our religion was hugging and kissing each other—a boy being unashamed to kiss his father on the lips and parents who showed affection in front of anyone. Our only doctrine had been "Do unto others as you would have them do unto you." So why did the Demon invade my psyche when I was eighteen years old? My only hope, as I prayed in that field, was to get rid of him once and for all. I covered all topics—everything and everyone whom I could possibly have wronged, including God, of course—and I asked for forgiveness. But in another part of my brain, I was screaming, "FORGIVENESS FOR WHAT?" I had no idea, but the strength of that absurdity couldn't pierce the armor of my compulsion. When I finished praying, I got up and walked home.

My mother, my father, and my pregnant sister, Corinne, were all waiting in the living room, dressed in their robes. From the expression on their faces, I thought that someone had died. My mother started crying. My father spoke first:

"We called the police—they just left here. Do you know what

time it is? It's three o'clock in the morning! Where were you? What in God's name were you doing?"

I couldn't bring myself to say, "I was praying, Daddy—I was lying in a field, praying to God to forgive me." And if he had said, "Forgive you for WHAT?" I would have said, "I don't know!" and he would have say, "For eight hours? Are you nuts?" . . . and he would have been right. So I mumbled something about having fallen asleep in a field because I was so tired. Then I apologized to all of them and went to my bedroom.

chapter 5

MY HEART IS NOT IN THE HIGHLANDS.

I went to Europe that summer, traveling in whichever was the cheapest class on the *Queen Elizabeth* (the original one). It was only $360.00 round trip. I thought a change of everything might help me.

We were four men in a very small cabin. One of them—an Englishman who was returning from India—told me about a heavenly place in the Highlands of Scotland, called the Isle of Skye . . . "just goats and sheep, eating their way through the small mountains. Plenty of bed-and-breakfast places to stay in." After I arrived in London, I decided to go to the Isle of Skye.

The little village of Portree sat at the edge of the water, where small boats came to dock. It *was* heavenly. Untouched. A simple place of original purity.

Up the cobblestoned street, near the beautiful old post office, stood a small outdoor urinal for travelers who had just arrived. I went in to relieve myself. Scribbled on the wall, in large black letters that faced me as I peed, I saw:

FUCK YOU

On my way back to London, I had to stop overnight in the town of Inverness, which was considered the entrance to the Highlands. After the sun went down, I wandered through the town, eating some fish-and-chips, and then returned to my small hotel room. I got on my knees and prayed for my usual request, which was to be forgiven for something that I didn't know I did, and then I took out a notepad and wrote my first poem.

> *Across three thousand miles of sea*
> *and through strange England's smiling,*
>
> *and into a wee Scots Highland town*
> *there is a lad who's crying.*
>
> *Oh fool the world, he could, he could,*
> *a man at twenty years . . .*
>
> *but all alone in that Highland town*
> *there is a boy in tears.*

In my senior year at Iowa, I played John Proctor in Arthur Miller's *The Crucible*. During the dress rehearsal, near the end of the play, I was standing in "a prison" and being asked to sign my name to a false document. My subconscious took over again—as it had once before, when I was sixteen, playing Willy Loman in *Death of a*

Salesman. I suddenly burst out with the lines: "BECAUSE IT IS MY NAME! BECAUSE I CANNOT HAVE ANOTHER IN MY LIFE!"

I'm sure every actor who has played John Proctor has burst out with great force—fake or real—when saying those lines, but they came out of me with so much emotion that it startled me and everyone else who was in the theater. Where the emotion came from, I hadn't a clue. Not at that time, anyway.

My wife in the play was a lovely actress named Joan. We had a date almost every Saturday night, in the home where she baby-sat for the same family. When the baby fell asleep, Joan and I would nestle into an overstuffed chair and watch *George Goble* on television. We kissed during the commercials. No breasts, no penis. Joan was a good actress and a very good singer. She said she was going to go to New York right after college, to "try her luck." Each time I kissed her good night, I'd say, "See you in New York!"

chapter 6

A YANK AT THE OLD VIC

After I graduated from Iowa in 1955 I got accepted at the Old Vic Theatre School, in Bristol, England. I wanted to go there because I felt deficient in all the physical techniques and the Old Vic offered courses in singing, movement, voice and speech, ballet exercise, Swedish gymnastics, and fencing. I took my Stanislavsky and my compulsion with me. I'd been acting since I was thirteen and praying compulsively since I was eighteen. I started to wonder if the compulsion would be with me for the rest of my life. Pain, then pleasure; pleasure, then pain.

On my way to England, on the *Queen Elizabeth* again, I met a young Indian girl named Romy who had been studying in New York and was returning to London. We hit it off very well, and I began questioning her about the philosophy of desirelessness.

"Well," she said, "in my religion we believe that life is full of suffering, and it's all caused by desire. And the only way to stop this
suffering is through enlightenment, so that we can end this sort of
endless cycle of births and deaths."

"And do you really want to stop desiring?"

"Well," she said, "I wish I could, but—" and she started to gig-
gle "—but I'm not strong enough to do that, because I'm enjoying
myself too much." And she giggled again.

When I got to Bristol, I stayed at the YMCA for a few days and
then found a very reasonable boardinghouse, run by a warm and
friendly Austrian lady. She was divorced and had her three children living with her. The cost to me was £11 per week—breakfast,
dinner, and lodging included—which came to $31.24 per week. If
you were lucky enough to find such a place today, it would cost
$324 per week. School was a fifteen-minute walk from the house.

The Old Vic school was located in three Victorian houses, all
stuck together, and offered a two-year course. I was one of two
Americans at the school; the other students were English.

Whenever I did a scene from Shakespeare in my acting class,
the principal of the school, Duncan Ross, would say, "You're
breaking the back of the meter, dear boy."

"I'm what?"

"Shakespeare wrote in iambic pentameter, and you're not paying any attention to it."

"Mr. Ross, I want my acting to come from a real human being. . . . I don't want to sound like a poetry professor."

"But you can't break the back of the meter, dear boy. You're acting some of the greatest lines every written, and they're written in
iambic pentameter . . . a long followed by a short, or a short followed by a long. . . . 'If *music be* the *food* of *love*, play *on*.' . . . Do
you see, dear boy?"

I liked Mr. Ross, but I wanted to punch him every time he said, "Dear boy."

Victor Shargai—the other American student—got tickets for the two of us to see Sir John Gielgud in *Much Ado About Nothing,* at Stratford-upon-Avon. Victor had written a note to Sir John, requesting a short meeting after the show, which Sir John graciously allowed. We went backstage when the play ended, and, after saying how wonderful we thought he was, I took a deep breath.

"Sir John, my acting teacher at the Old Vic school keeps telling me that I'm breaking the back of the meter whenever I do a scene from Shakespeare. Do you think about meter and iambic pentameter when you're on stage, acting those beautiful lines?"

"No, I don't think about such things when I'm acting. Shakespeare takes care of most of the work. . . . If you have a good ear, the poetry will come out. If you don't have a good ear, it won't much matter what you do."

When Victor and I got back to school the next day, the principal was waiting for me.

"Well, what did the Master have to say?"

I told him what the Master had to say.

As long as I was with the other students in class, I felt safe. They all loved it when I took on the principal and argued with him, for hours, even after the school day was over. But when I was alone, I was vulnerable. The Demon would arrive and prod me until I bled from guilt—as if I had killed someone and left him to die alone. I no longer thought of my praying as holy . . . I hated it.

Of all the courses, fencing was my favorite. I won the All School Fencing Championship after only six months. No first-year student had ever done that before. All my years of "pretend sword fighting," and all the Errol Flynn movies I'd seen, had paid off. But when the principal got around to teaching more advanced acting—for example, how to laugh onstage by letting all the air out of your gut and creating a gagging effect, or how to find a chair onstage without looking down, by feeling for it with your toe or heel—I decided to leave. I knew I would be drafted shortly after I got back to the States (this was near the end of Compulsory Military Training), and I wanted to study where they taught Stanislavsky.

My sister had started acting classes at the HB Studio in New York, which was run by Herbert Berghof and his wife, Uta Hagen. Corinne invited me to come to New York and live with her and her family in Queens, so I drove from Milwaukee and enrolled at the HB Studio that summer.

chapter 7

SHADES OF GRAY

I was drafted into the army on September 10, 1956. All I took with me were some underwear, a few pair of socks, and *Dear Theo*—the letters of van Gogh to his brother Theo. At the end of Basic Training, I was assigned to the medical corps and sent to Fort Sam Houston, in San Antonio, Texas, for eight weeks of medical training.

While I was at Fort Sam, I helped the officers' wives stage-manage a variety show that they had written. The wife in charge of the production was married to a colonel, who just happened to be the commanding officer of Fort Sam Houston. At the end of my eight weeks—when I was about to be given the orders that would station me somewhere in the world for the next year and eight months—a letter from the commanding officer instructed the office in charge of issuing orders to allow me to pick any post that was open, anywhere in the country. I was glad I had helped the commanding officer's wife. I chose Valley Forge Army Hospital, in Phoenixville, Pennsylvania which was the closest post to New York City.

When I arrived at Valley Forge, I was given a choice of work: sterilization of equipment, tubercular ward, etc. I chose the Neuropsychiatric hospital, which was across the road. I imagined that the things I would see there might relate more to acting than any of the other choices. I wasn't wrong.

On my first day at work, I was shown a short film called *Shades of Gray,* which showed the mental health of all of us as being at some stage of gray—none of us being completely white or black. If stress is too great, the gray becomes darker. If the gray becomes too dark, that person needs to be institutionalized. Watching the film, I felt a sense of relief that I really didn't understand.

I was assigned to a "locked ward," which meant that the patients were locked in, with bars on the windows, to protect them and to keep them from escaping. All the young soldiers, and some older ones, had had psychotic breakdowns, not from war stress—this was peacetime—but from other kinds of stress. Every patient arrived in an ambulance, wearing a straitjacket—that was regulation— because some of these men had become violent when their emotional dam broke.

One twenty-year-old boy who had lived on a farm for the first nineteen-and-a-half years of his life had a psychotic breakdown on his first day in the army when some burly sergeant yelled, "Hey, farm boy—lift your fucking duffel bag and get in the fucking line!" By the time they brought him to us, he was catatonic.

My main job on the day shift was to help administer electroshock therapy, which meant holding the patient down while the doctor induced a grand mal seizure. I had a terrible time emotionally for three or four weeks, until I started to see the good that often came from it—perhaps only temporarily. The analogy the doctors gave us was that it was like lifting up a car that was stuck in the snow because its wheels kept spinning, digging the car in deeper. When the troubled mind is no longer in the same rut, maybe it will take a new path.

The evening shift was my favorite. I helped escort the patients from the locked ward to a Red Cross dance, three times a week. It was held in a reception hall on the ground floor. No bars on the windows. A busload of young girls—all volunteers—came in from town, which was two miles away, to dance with the patients. The other corpsmen and I were not allowed to dance with these young girls. The Teamsters always provided a small band, which played popular standards. I was tempted to break the rules and ask one of the young ladies to dance. I thought of what might happen if a nurse came in and started reprimanding me:

"Silberman, don't you know the rules?"

"Mam, I was dancing with this young lady to show this patient that there's absolutely nothing to be afraid of."

But I was too chicken to ever try it. There was one young patient who played bridge with me at these dances, when we could find two other bridge players. He was so normal that I couldn't understand why on earth he was put into a mental hospital, let alone into a locked ward.

"Dick," I asked, "what the hell are you doing here? You're saner than I am."

"When I was attending class at Officers' Training," he said, "it took me 5 minutes to straighten all the books on my desk. They had to be stacked properly, all facing in the same direction and with all the edges touching each other in a correct way. The next day it took me 15 minutes to straighten my books, then 30 minutes, then 45 . . . and by that time the class was over."

Another young man, named Roger, was terrified of stepping on cracks. He was also terrified of dancing with any of the girls. The few times he did ask a girl to dance, he got a horrible headache and begged me to take him back to his bed. Once, while we were walking along the wooden corridor, on the way back to the ward—with him zigzagging all over the place to avoid stepping on cracks—I said, "Tell me something, Roger: what do you think is going to happen to you if you do—just accidentally—step on a crack?"

"I don't know," he said. "But please don't make me do it."

Another patient would go into the latrine every night and wrap a thin white string around his penis. That fellow I stayed clear of. Sure, I wanted to ask him, "Why the hell are you wrapping string around your penis?" But he was so sick I was afraid my question might set him off.

Of all these young men, the one who got to me the most was the patient who knelt down each morning in front of the television set—blocking the view of all the other patients who were watching *Amos and Andy*—and began praying . . . to the monitor? Or Amos? Or Kingfisher? Or God? (*Hold on here,* I thought. *You're getting into my territory.*)

That's when the heavenly thought first occurred to me that maybe I wasn't called on by God to do some special and sacrificial thing. . . . Maybe I was just sick.

We were given two days off each week. The other soldiers wanted Saturdays and Sundays; I wanted Mondays and Tuesdays, because New York was an hour-and-a-half train ride away and that meant I could attend acting class at the HB Studio every Monday night. Corinne and her husband, Gil, said that I could stay with them and their baby, in their small apartment in Queens, on my two days off. All my friends at Valley Forge loved me for never putting in for weekends.

The following November—while I was in Queens on my two

days off—I got a phone call from my uncle Irv, in Milwaukee, telling me that my mother had just died. I wasn't surprised, because she had been so ill. They had discovered that she had breast cancer the year before, but they couldn't treat her because her heart wasn't strong enough. She died of heart failure.

I called my sergeant at Valley Forge Hospital and told him about my mother. He was usually pretty gruff or stoic, but on this occasion he was very kind and said that I could go to Milwaukee for the funeral and that I should just come back when I was ready. So I flew to Milwaukee, and at the cemetery I got into an argument with two of my uncles, who told me that—according to the Jewish religion—I couldn't be a pallbearer for my own mother. I grabbed one of the handles that held up the casket, and I walked along, with five other men. We set her down in her grave.

Now here's a strange thing: about a month later I bought my first condom. I didn't know quite how to use it; it seemed tricky to me. I mean, exactly when do you put it on and do you ask the woman for help and when do you take it off? Of course, a more important question would have been, "Who the hell is this woman you're talking to who's going to help you put a piece of rubber over your penis?"

By the way, I wasn't praying as much anymore.

chapter 8

DON JUAN IN NEW YORK

"See you in New York!"

I said that to Joan so many times when we had our baby-sitting
dates on Saturday nights, watching *George Goble*, kissing during
the commercials, standing in the doorway for a last good-night
kiss, and then . . . "See you in New York!"

Joan had written to me once while I was in the army, just to let
me know that she was studying singing at the Ansonia Hotel and
that I could see her in New York. She gave me her address.

I hadn't seen Joan for over a year, and now I'm riding on a train
from North Philadelphia to New York with a condom packed as
carefully as I could place it in my wallet, and it was burning a hole
in my brain because I kept thinking, *What if there's a tiny hole in the
condom because I inserted it next to my plastic driver's license and the
train is jostling back and forth and side to side and up and down? Jesus,*

it sounds like the condom is making love already. On its own! I wish it could—then I wouldn't have to figure out how to do it. Twenty-two years old and still a virgin? Why? Could it be that if I made love—not hugging and kissing, but actually putting my penis inside a woman's vagina—I would somehow be betraying my mother? That's crazy. Or is it because God has more important things for me to do than to fuck around with pleasure? Oh, excuse me—that's not crazy? I feel like I'm talking to one of the patients on the locked ward. Maybe I'm the one who's crazy. Maybe I should be on the locked ward with them. But if I can say that—then I'm not crazy. That much I learned at the hospital. Acting seems so much easier than life. When I'm on stage, I feel safe. "They' can't get me." (Careful, son . . . you're talking crazy again.) But onstage, everyone listens to me and watches me and—if I'm any good— applauds me. And when I'm taking my bow, I have the belief that I've earned my feeling of grace—as if God were saying, "You did something worthwhile, so I won't punish you . . . for a few days.

Then I heard the conductor shout, "NEW YORK NEXT! LAST STOP—NEW YORK CITY!"

*   *   *

ME: Do you know who Katharine Cornell was?

MARGIE: Never mind who Katharine Cornell was—did you make love to Joan?

ME: I don't know.

MARGIE: What does that mean?

ME: No kissing, no hugging—

MARGIE: Wait a minute, *Mister* Wilder—kissing is what you majored in. Don't tell me there was no kissing.

ME: Yes, we did a little mitsy-bitsy "Hello, how are you?" kind of kissing, but there wasn't any *real* kissing. No touching. NO LAUGHING! I think that was the biggest problem. I'm guessing Joan was also a virgin—I don't know. I thought I was the only virgin in New York. But I think she was just as afraid of messing up the "ideal" as I was: "If you're too aggressive, what will she/he think of me?"

MARGIE: What happened?

ME: We got into her bedroom. She turned off the lights and took off her clothes and lay down on this little narrow bed. No talking. I think she must have been as nervous as I was. Then I took off my clothes, trying to hide the condom from her because I thought it wasn't romantic. I held the condom in one hand while I tried to get out of my pants and underwear. Then I put the condom on my penis and got into bed with her. All I could think was, *If I lose my erection, will the condom fall off?* When I felt her naked body against my legs, I figured that I had better put my penis into her vagina while I still had the erection. I got halfway in and . . . boom!

MARGIE: You shot your wad.

ME: Thanks for putting it so delicately.

MARGIE: You're welcome. And after "boom"?

ME: I'm an actor. . . . I acted a migraine headache. I told her I should never have tried making love under the circumstances, but I didn't want to disappoint her, and how sorry I was, but I just felt as if my head were going to burst, and that I'd better go. I remembered thinking of poor Roger at Valley Forge—the patient who got those terrible headaches every time he danced with a girl. I had much more compassion for him now. Joan was very sympathetic. Maybe she was relieved, I don't know. We sort of kissed good night, and then I left, feeling like a fool. That was five years ago, and I still feel like a fool. So, how do you think I did?

MARGIE: Well, I wouldn't call you Don Juan, but . . . not bad, for the first time. So what about Katharine Cornell?

ME: I've heard that she used to be so nervous before a performance that she had to throw up . . . then she'd step out on stage and be brilliant.

STEPPING INTO LIFE

I got out of the army two years to the day after I was drafted and went to New York. My time in the army qualified me for unemployment insurance—thirty-five dollars a week. That was to pay for rent, food, and entertainment. Not much, but it helped, and I had saved a little from my monthly salary at Valley Forge. I found a tiny loft in the artificial flower district on Thirtieth Street, near Lord and Taylor's department store, for one hundred dollars a month.

I got a scholarship to the HB Studio, so I was able to study acting full-time: Monday nights with Herbert Berghof and Thursday afternoons with Uta Hagen. I'd rehearse for two or three weeks with one acting partner during the day, and a different scene with a different acting partner during the evenings.

The odd thing is, I never did comedy scenes in class. I knew that comedy was my talent, but I wanted to learn "Stanislavsky"— *real* acting—so I always chose dramatic scenes. Of course, my thinking was schoolboy logic. There wasn't any reason I couldn't have learned just as much by doing comedy scenes—which are all the funnier if done by actors who are playing them for *real.* I just didn't know that yet.

In Uta's class I did a scene from a Kafka short story with a lovely girl named Jessie. The work was good, but Jessie was better. She became my first actual girlfriend. I suppose it happened because we got to know each other before there was any physical intimacy. She worked as a freelance fashion designer, so we would rehearse at all hours, and then have either lunch or dinner together—something very inexpensive. We also laughed a lot. I couldn't afford my tiny loft any longer—cheap as it was—so Jessie asked me to move in with her.

Physically, it was "Heaven on a stick"—for me, since I was the stick. But I didn't know how to make her as happy as she was making me—how to touch her, where to touch her, with my finger, with my tongue. Eventually her frustration drove us apart. I felt like an imbecile again.

The compulsion came and went, but not so often anymore, and not in the same way. Now it would take something special to set it off, and it was always something I'd read or a picture I'd seen— someone who was doing something noble and unselfish to help others, and usually the noble person was making a sacrifice. Compulsion is doing; obsession is thinking. Instead of compulsive praying, the Demon—when he did come—took the form of obsessive thinking.

BEING A PROFESSIONAL MEANS YOU GET PAID.

I got my first professional acting job playing the Second Officer in Herbert Berghof's production of Twelfth Night, at the Cambridge Drama Festival. We performed in a huge tent alongside the Charles River. Herbert wanted me, I'm sure, because he needed a good fencing choreographer for the comic duel. And I was a good one.

Then the famous Cuban director José Quintero asked me to stay on and do the fencing choreography for Macbeth, with Jason Robards, Jr., and Siobhan McKenna. During rehearsals—when Mr. Robards was exhausted after a heavy emotional scene—he'd sit in the theater and watch the other actors rehearse scenes he wasn't in, while he tried to catch his breath. It was during those short rest periods that I would go over the choreography of his sword fights, each of us holding a pencil instead of a sword, and going through all the movements in miniature.

chapter 9

THE WORST OF TIMES, THE BEST OF TIMES

When I returned to New York, I got a job teaching fencing at the Circle in the Square Theater . . . forty dollars a week, under the table.

I also got a job working for "Chauffeurs Unlimited: We Drive Your Car." I earned two dollars an hour, plus tips. The owner of the company had polio and conducted all business from his apartment. He knew I was studying or rehearsing almost every day, and he told me that I could refuse any job, anytime, if it interfered with my "real" work. More than that I couldn't ask. The clients would usually want to go to the theater and then to some restaurant for dinner afterwards, so after I left them at their theater I drove to the HB Studio and watched an acting class for a couple of hours. I met Mary at one of these classes.

Mary was English. I'm always drawn to English people, man or woman—I suppose because of my days at the Bristol Old Vic. Besides being English, Mary was also beautiful—in classical terms. I don't mean sexy—I wasn't at all physically attracted. Her beauty was fragile, in the way that Greta Garbo was fragile and beautiful. She was also a wonderful actress. To top it off, she was also a painter, so the cards were stacked against me.

After we had seen each other several times at the HB Studio, she heard that I had to get out of my temporary apartment. Mary said that I could stay with her for a few days, until I found something I could afford. What fools these mortals be. I moved in with Mary.

She had twin beds, at right angles to each other. One night, after all the lights were out, I heard a gentle invitation to join her in bed. I thought that she would think that I didn't find her attractive, which of course was the truth, but I didn't want to hurt her feelings in *that* way. So I joined her. I wouldn't say the rest was history . . . although in a way it was.

Several days later I saw an ad for a studio apartment that sounded very reasonable. I told Mary that I was going to look at it. Tears came to her eyes.

"Why do you have to go?"

"Well . . . what do you mean? You said I could stay with you for a few days, till I could find something else. . . . Don't you remember?"

"But why leave?"

"But I have to find my own place, Mary."

"Why?"

"I don't think it's healthy this way—I mean, emotionally—for either of us."

"Don't you like me?"

"Of course I like you. . . . What are you talking about?"

The tears flowed from her eyes like raindrops.

"So why do you have to go?"

I did look at that apartment; it was terrible. Sunlight got lost trying to find its way in. No wonder it was so cheap.

Several days later, while Mary and I were having dinner, I got a phone call from a friend of mine from class. He told me that his girlfriend was pregnant.

"What are you going to do?" I asked.

"I'm going to marry her," he said. "I think I have to."

After I hung up, I told Mary about the call, and she said, "You'd be out of here faster than a speeding bullet if that ever happened to us." What possessed me, I don't know—some kind of idiotic gallantry, I suppose—but I answered, "No I wouldn't." Mary stared at me for several seconds. I held her gaze. Then she came over and kissed me. We were engaged that night.

Mary worked at the British Information Service in Rockefeller Center. I would meet her during her tea break in the afternoons, and we'd have a quick kiss. I thought, perhaps, married life could be wonderful.

We were married that July. I borrowed a friend's old Buick, and we drove to a justice of the peace in Suffern County, New York.

After the four-minute ceremony—a policeman and a postal worker were our witnesses—we drove to Mystic, Connecticut, for our honeymoon. We were no sooner out of the justice's driveway than the battles began: which route to take—inland or the coast, which diner to stop at for breakfast, which music to listen to, which motel to stop at that night, which restaurant to have dinner in. It wasn't a romantic honeymoon; it never was romantic from that time on.

WHAT DO ACTORS WANT?

Apart from fame and fortune and all the whipped cream that goes with them, which very few actors ever achieve—what do actors really want, artistically? To be great actors? Yes, but you can't buy talent, so it's best to leave the word "great" out of it—it just gets you into trouble. I think to be *believed*—onstage or on-screen—is the one hope that all actors share. Which one of us, anywhere in the world, doesn't yearn to be believed when the audience is watching?

I'd been studying with Herbert Berghof and Uta Hagen for three years now—two of them while I was still in the army—but I felt that there was something basic missing, something less intellectual than what they offered. I wanted to know how to reach that area of the subconscious that I had reached, by accident, in *Death of a Salesman* and *The Crucible*.

Stanislavsky called two of his main tools Actions and Objectives, and that's what I was being taught—that the character you're playing must *want* something (an Objective) and then he needed Actions to accomplish his Objective. Just as an example, let's suppose that I'm really smitten with the beautiful Frenchwoman who lives upstairs and that I desperately *want* her to love me. To achieve my Objective, I might:

1. Try to nonchalantly hold her hand when we meet on the street.
2. Say something in French as we pass each other on the stairs.
3. Affect a limp as we meet on the sidewalk, in hopes that she'll now look at me in a special way.
4. Invite her to dinner in my apartment, but before she arrives, arrange piles of her favorite flower in every place where she might sit.

I was exhausting myself with Actions and Objectives, and I didn't know if the problem lay in my shortcomings or the process itself. Twenty seconds before I was about to do a scene in class, I would still be searching for my Objective, thinking that if only I could find the right one, it would solve all my acting problems. I even started thinking that the greater my Objective, the greater my acting would be.

One of my closest friends was—and still is—Charles Grodin. He had recently started studying with Lee Strasberg. When we were both on unemployment, Chuck and I used to meet on summer evenings, drink our Pepsis, and walk along the East River, talking about life and love—but mostly about acting. One night I asked Chuck what Strasberg said about Actions and Objectives. He said he'd never heard him mention those words. A month later I began studying with Lee Strasberg in his private class.

STRASBERG'S CLASS

Each class started in the same way, with "sense memory" exercises, in which you tried to recall one of your sharpest memories of smell, hearing, taste, sight, or touch.

Every Thursday afternoon six students, out of thirty in the class, would sit in chairs onstage and try to get into a relaxed position—a position in which you could possibly fall asleep—while the remainder of the class was watching. In the first weeks we all started out with an exercise that was very simple, such as holding a cup of hot coffee or tea, trying to feel the weight of the cup, and then actually taking a drink . . . except of course that there was no cup, only the imaginary one you were holding, which was filled with imaginary hot coffee or tea that you were trying to taste.

Then we advanced to recalling some physical pain. I sat on my chair, and after I felt relaxed, I imagined that I was sitting in a dentist's chair, trying to recall having my tooth drilled. In this exercise I was more successful than any of the others, perhaps because I had had so much experience in the dentist's chair. After three or four minutes of recalling that drill—how it looked and how it smelled and even how it tasted as it bore its way into my tooth—I felt the pain so sharply that tears came to my eyes. Now I understood what a sense memory was.

Of course, the whole idea of the thing was not to be able to recall hot tea or a dentist's drill, but rather to recall something that could be used on stage in other ways. For example: You're in a play, on the witness stand, accused of a murder that you didn't commit. The prosecuting attorney is grilling you. You're in the hot seat, so to speak. If the actual situation and the author's words don't start your emotional motor going, you might try a sense memory of being in a steam bath—feeling the heat and tasting the salt as the sweat pours out of you—so long as you avoid any giveaway physical actions that are strictly steam bath behavior. Hopefully, the audience will see someone who seems to be sweating bullets because of the questions the prosecuting attorney is asking.

During these months in Strasberg's classes, I used to sneak into the balcony of The Actors Studio and watch him give critiques to members. A very talented actor named Gerald Hiken had just done his first scene for Lee Strasberg. After the scene was over, Strasberg said, "Tell us what you were working on." Gerald said, "I just wanted to show you how I normally work—using Actions, Objectives, Conditions, Obstacles . . . all the things I was taught in classes with Uta Hagen."

Then Strasberg illuminated the mystery I had been wrestling with for many years. He said, "You did very well, Gerald, because we got it. We could see everything you worked on—all the Actions and Objectives and all the rest of it. But at the Studio we believe that if you have a relaxed body and a relaxed mind, and if you can believe that the situation the character is in is *actually happening to you,* then all those other things you were talking about are going to happen by themselves, only not in an intellectual way, but in a more natural, organic way. And if they don't, then we have certain tools we use that might help you. But they're not intellectual tools."

These critiques that I snuck in to hear were for professional, working actors. Now more than ever, I wanted to get into the Studio.

THE ACTORS STUDIO

To get into the Studio you had to pass a final audition, judged by Cheryl Crawford, Lee Strasberg, and Elia Kazan. At least two out of those three had to vote yes. No discussion. In those days, it was very difficult to become a member.

Mary got into the Studio in the May finals. Six months later she did a scene with me for the January finals. I didn't do a comedy scene, of course—I was too stupid to realize my strengths. Instead, I did a dramatic scene from a short story. But there was a certain innocence about the way I played the scene, and I think it was that quality that won the jury over. I passed the audition. Only two people out of twelve hundred got into the Studio that January.

A few days later I became curious to find out how the three judges voted. One evening after I finished rehearsing a scene at the Studio, I peeked into the secretary's unlocked desk: Cheryl Crawford and Elia Kazan voted yes . . . but not Strasberg.

I had to choose a name, fast, before being introduced to all the members of the Studio. I didn't think "Jerry Silberman in *Macbeth*" had the right ring to it.

I went to my sister and brother-in-law's apartment for dinner. With them was a screenwriter friend of theirs by the name of David Zelag Goodman. He talked so fast that, as I listened to him, I had the urge to gently wipe the foam from his mouth with a hanky. When David heard that I needed a stage name, he started with *A* and worked his way through the alphabet, ripping off names faster than I thought anyone could think and speak at the same time. When he got to *W* and said, "Wilder," the bell went off . . . Thornton Wilder . . . *Our Town.* I wanted to be "Wilder."

After settling on the last name, I knew that I wanted only one syllable for my first name. "Gene" came from *Look Homeward Angel,* by Thomas Wolfe. The hero's name was Eugene, but everyone who loved him called him Gene.

There was another reason I chose Gene as a first name. When I was a little boy, during World War II, there was a big family dinner for a distant relative who had just flown in from Europe on a three-week leave after flying thirty-three missions over Germany. He was wearing his tattered leather flight jacket, and he was very handsome, and his name was Gene. I had never heard Gene used as a man's name before.

Margie made her usual timely interruption.

"By the way, what was your mother's name?"

I felt like the biggest dummy in New York. After an embarrassed pause I finally said, "Jeanne."

On my first morning as a member of The Actors Studio, Lee Strasberg addressed the audience of actors: "The second actor who passed, and who is now a member of The Actors Studio, is—"

Strasberg was used to calling me Jerry Silberman in his private class. He looked down at the white index card he was holding and then said.

"Gene Wilder!"

As everyone applauded, I lifted myself halfway off my seat and gave a little nod.

"NO SIR!" Strasberg bellowed. "Here, if we're going to take a bow, we take a bow! I'll start again." He repeated, "Gene Wilder!"

I stood up, tall, and acknowledged the applause from an audience made up of so many actors I had seen in movies and on television.

My first scene at The Actors Studio was from a short story by J. D. Salinger called "For Esmé, with Love and Squalor." When the scene was over, Strasberg said a few words that stuck in the artistic half of my brain:

"We know you're sensitive. You're always sensitive. You're too goddamn sensitive! So you don't have to show us that you're sensitive. Show us some other colors—something we don't know."

Then he said, "When you were standing at the refrigerator in your scene, trying to decide whether you should pick up the telephone . . . something very interesting was starting to happen . . . and then you just let it drop. Why'd you do that?"

"I knew I could act that part of the scene, Lee. That's my kind of stuff, so I didn't work on it. I thought I should concentrate on what I didn't know how to do."

He said, "I got news for you: If you don't know how you're going to act some part of the script—work on what you *do* know. Build up your confidence a little bit. That will help you find what you don't know."

ROOTS

Mary had auditioned for an English play called *Roots,* by Arnold Wesker, which was going to be done off Broadway and directed by a first-time director named Mark Rydell. (After *Roots* Mark went to Hollywood and began making beautiful films. *On Golden Pond* was one of them.)

Mark was very impressed by Mary. He was also looking for someone to play her character's husband, Frankie Bryant. I asked Mary if she could get me an audition. She asked, and they said yes. Mary helped me with my North Country English accent. She also suggested little touches of authenticity, like sticking a handkerchief up the sleeve of my borrowed costume jacket, since I was supposed to be something of a country bumpkin. From that time on, whenever I did an audition, I always wore some suggestion of a costume that fitted the character.

I did my audition for Mark Rydell. He liked it, and Mary and I were cast in the play as husband and wife.

The opening night was filled with dignitaries, including Mark's agent, a magnificent lady named Lily Veidt. She was the Jewish widow of the famous German actor Conrad Veidt, who had left Germany with Lily to escape Hitler. He brought Lily to Hollywood, where he was cast as the Nazi colonel in *Casablanca.* When Conrad Veidt died in 1950, Louis B. Mayer talked Lily into becoming a theatrical agent. The morning after *Roots* opened, I got a call from Lily's secretary, asking if I had representation. When I went to her office, she asked if I would like her to represent me in New York. She became my first agent and a second mother to me.

The executive producer of a television program called *The Play of the Week* had seen me in *Roots* and offered me the part of a cockney Englishman in Maxwell Anderson's *Wingless Victory,* starring Eartha Kitt and Hugh O'Brian.

Irene Mayer Selznick—who had produced *A Streetcar Named Desire* on Broadway—saw me in *Wingless Victory* and asked me to come to her office. She had the strange notion that I might be right for the part of the Dutch valet in Graham Greene's *The Complaisant Lover*, starring Michael Redgrave, which she was going to produce on Broadway.

I went to the Netherlands Information Service and took two lessons on how to speak with a Dutch accent. Then I had to audition for the director, a revered Englishman named Glen Byam Shaw. Irene Selznick was a smart cookie; she arranged for Mr. Shaw to audition the twenty other actors who were reading for the same part, and then she had me come in last. I had rented a valet's jacket from a costume house, memorized the lines, got the part, and won the Clarence Derwent Award for "Best Performance by an Actor in a Nonfeatured Role." Sounds so simple, but I was always good with accents, and by that time I knew how to act in comedy using the same method as I did for drama, which is . . . make it real.

chapter 10

MOTHER COURAGE

January 1963

Jerome Robbins was going to direct Bertolt Brecht's play *Mother Courage* on Broadway, with Anne Bancroft as the star.

Mr. Robbins wanted to audition as many actors from the Studio as he could, and since Cheryl Crawford was producing the play, it was easy. (She was the one who got me into the Studio, along with Elia Kazan.)

I read for the small, but very good part of Swiss Cheese, Mother Courage's son. I memorized the scene I was supposed to read, as I always did, and found a "character jacket." The audition went so well that Mr. Robbins asked me to come back the next day and read again. That audition went so well that he asked me to study the part of the Chaplain, which was one of the leading roles.

I memorized the scene he wanted me to read, found another

character jacket, and also brought a prop (a hammer or a broom, I forget which) so that I could be doing something instead of just standing there, saying lines.

The reading went so well that Mr. Robbins asked me to come back the next day and audition again. This turned out to be a habit of Jerome Robbins's—to keep actors reading, so that he could be "sure," and also, I'm sure, so that he could get ideas for how to direct certain scenes. (According to Actors Equity, you're supposed to pay an actor after three readings, which Mr. Robbins never did.)

After my fifth reading I was told that I would have to do one more *final* audition. The competition for the role was between me and Gerald Hiken—the wonderful actor whose first scene at The Actors Studio I had snuck in to watch from the balcony. By this time my confidence had dropped a few notches. The horrible trap is that an actor tries to remember what he or she did that impressed the director originally, and, unfortunately, the actor starts imitating what he thought he did. Nevertheless, after my sixth audition, I got the part. Barbara Harris was cast as the Prostitute, and Zohra Lampert was cast as the mute daughter of Mother Courage.

Rehearsals were a little strained. Mr. Robbins thought that the best way to get us into Brecht's Communist/Socialist way of thinking was for all of us to play Monopoly during our lunch hour. I should have known that there was trouble ahead.

We opened previews at the Martin Beck Theater to a packed house. I had a rousing and funny scene toward the end of the first act, after which Mother Courage and her daughter and I pushed Mother Courage's wagon to our next destination (on a revolving stage), accompanied by some thrilling music. Before the curtain could come down, the audience burst into applause. Anne and Zohra and I were filled with joy. But Mr. Robbins cut the heart of the scene the next day. He said, "That isn't what Brecht wants. It's the intellectual ideas that he's trying to get across, not the conventional emotion that we get in American plays." (My father would have said, "Was you there, Charley?")

Jerome Robbins found a patsy in every production—someone he could pick on if he was frustrated with how things were going. (Many famous directors have been guilty of the same habit—Otto Preminger and John Dexter, to name two.)

Robbins had selected a wonderful actor by the name of Eugene Roche to be his patsy. One afternoon, when everything Mr. Robbins was doing seemed to make things worse, he started in on Eugene in front of the rest of the cast. We all had to stand there and listen to Jerry Robbins railing and belittling—until he crossed the line. Eugene, who was a devout Catholic with five children, stood up and said:

"Listen, you little fuck—if you insult me one more time, I'm going to come over there and smash the teeth out of your fucking face."

From that time on, Eugene Roche became Jerome Robbins's favorite actor.

After the previews began, Anne Bancroft's boyfriend came to pick her up each night, after the show. The boyfriend's name was Mel Brooks.

When I met Mel for the first time he was wearing a black pea jacket, of the kind made famous by the merchant marines. Mel said, "You know, they used to call these urine jackets, but they didn't sell." Anne and I burst out laughing. She's probably still his best audience.

I was terribly miscast in Mother Courage. Most of us were—especially Jerome Robbins. Despite Anne's Academy Award that year for The Miracle Worker, Mother Courage closed after three months.

When the closing notice went up, Mel asked if I would like to spend a weekend with him and Anne on Fire Island. He said that he had thirty pages of a screenplay he was writing and that he wanted to read it to us. It was called *Springtime for Hitler*.

I went to visit them on a weekend in June. Mel met me at the dock where the ferry comes in, and then he and I went fishing off the surf for about an hour. After dinner Mel asked Anne and me to sit down, and then he began reading the first three scenes of *Springtime for Hitler*, almost verbatim as they eventually appeared on screen—except the title was later changed to *The Producers*. Anne and I loved it.

"So, would you like to play the part of Leo Bloom?"

"Oh, yes, I would."

"All right, now listen to me—don't take anything on Broadway or Off Broadway or anywhere else without checking with me first. Promise?"

"I promise."

That September I was offered *One Flew Over the Cuckoo's Nest*, to be produced on Broadway, Kirk Douglas starring, with Alex Segal directing. I was asked to play the part of Billie Bibbit, the young boy who stutters terribly and then commits suicide at the end of the play. I called Mel and told him the situation.

"Can you give them a two-week notice if you want to get out?"

"Two weeks? . . . Mel, I'm not a star. They might accept a four-week notice."

"All right, all right—we'll have to live with it."

UNEXPRESSED ANGER

I did get a provision in my contract that I could give a four-week notice if I wanted to get out of the play. I think I was good in *One*

Flew Over the Cuckoo's Nest, but I don't think I could have done the part nearly as well if I hadn't spent a year and a half at Valley Forge Army Hospital, on a locked ward, with all those poor fellows who were in the middle of psychotic breakdowns.

After three months there was still no word from Mel. I wasn't going to call him—I guessed that they must be having problems raising money for *Springtime for Hitler.*

Something basic had changed since the days when I would meet Mary at the British Information Service for a quick kiss. I tried to make a go of our physical and emotional life, but there was no response. Mary and I made love once every six months—like clockwork. Easy for me to say, I know, but affection is my middle name, and her affection for me had dried up.

That fall she was cast in a play with Jane Fonda and wore the same heavy angora sweater to rehearsals every day. The director came to me, privately, and said that the odor from her underarms was so strong that he and the other actors were having a hard time. He asked if I would say something to her. I did tell her, that evening, as gently as I could. She just said, "Oh, poof."

That spring Mary and I went to Ogunquit, Maine, to rehearse a workshop production of a new play. We stayed at a beautiful old inn that I knew from having worked at the Ogunquit Playhouse the summer before. This old house was a typical New England inn and had a small but lovely dining room. The only requirement for eating there was that men had to wear jackets and ladies had to wear a dress or a skirt—no pants. Mary refused to wear a dress or a skirt—she insisted on pants. So we walked into town most nights and ate at the local diner.

I'm not saying that the Demon came back because my wife refused to wear a dress. . . . I'm saying that I felt a rage that I didn't, or couldn't, express.

———

That summer Mary announced that she was going to Italy for six
A woman I had seen several times in the elevator was moving out
of her apartment. She had found something more to her liking on
the Upper East Side, and she could afford it. I'll call her Karla. She
was not a fragile beauty; she was a buxom redhead—not unattrac-
tive—and looked a little like a former wrestler. She must have
known that I was having troubles in my marriage because on the
day that she moved out she handed me a card with her new address and telephone number. When we shook hands good-bye,
she said, "If you ever get lonely, just give me a call."

I shook my head after she disappeared down the hall. Karla
would certainly be the last person in the world I'd ever call if I were
lonely. Of course, if she had been fragile, artistic, and blond . . .

Our apartment was on Thirty-third Street, off Lexington Avenue.
weeks to act in a play at Gian Carlo Menotti's Spoleto Festival. She
said she'd be back on September 5.

I went on a summer tour in a play called *The White House*, starring Helen Hayes. It had a good cast, and most of us had done the
play with her on Broadway that spring. She played the wife of
every president from George Washington to Woodrow Wilson,
and I played one or two lawyers, a college roommate, and Mary
Lincoln's son at her trial. The play didn't last very long on Broadway, but Miss Hayes liked it so much that she took a big cut in
salary and asked all of us to tour New England with her in the
summer.

I liked Helen Hayes—as an actress and as a person—but as well
as we all got along with her, none of us ever called her Helen, only
"Miss Hayes." I wanted to be a little more familiar, but she had an
aura about her from a world I had only read about.

When I got back to New York, I decided to give my marriage

one last chance. Mary was due back in ten days. I found a new apartment on Fifty-seventh and Third Avenue. It was only one room, but it was a big L-shaped room, with a little kitchenette, and it was new and clean, with sunlight pouring through the large window that overlooked Fifty-seventh Street. The rent was $150 a month, which was certainly reasonable, but also the limit of what I could afford.

I bought a new dining room table, made of raw pinewood, and I antiqued it myself. I'm not a very good carpenter, but this had more to do with painting than carpentry.

On the morning of September 5, I bought some flowers, placed them in a little vase in the center of the table, and took a shower. When I got out of the shower, a telegram arrived:

Staying in Italy another two weeks. Stop. Mary.

I had the urge to break something. I sat still for a long time, trying to think of what I could do to release the rage in me. Then I searched through my address book until I found what I was looking for: "If you should ever get lonely, just give me a call."

As I was about to knock on Karla's door, I heard a man talking in her apartment, and then I heard Karla's voice. I figured, *Well, a neighbor, a relative, who knows?* I knocked.

Karla came to the door. I saw what looked like a well-dressed businessman just finishing tucking in his shirt. He reached for his jacket, and Karla introduced us. I don't remember what his name was—I just remember the tucking in of his shirt.

The man said a polite good-bye, and Karla asked me to come in and make myself comfortable. (*What is this? Am I supposed to pay her?*)

She offered me some coffee and then invited me into her bedroom, as if we had arranged all of this beforehand. Karla started getting undressed. After a few awkward moments of standing there, I got undressed.

"You know," she said, "I've become something of a nymphomaniac lately." She followed this with a little laugh.

"It's just that, at this point in my life I get a little lonely. I hope you don't mind."

"Me? No, of course not." *(What in God's name am I saying? I sound like Woody Allen.)*

I got into bed with her and sort of kissed her, after which she put "it" inside. I guess you could have counted to seven or eight, and then boom.

I tried to be as polite as I could manage to be in what was an absurd situation. And actually, she was trying to be polite as well. I just wanted to get out of there. After several polite thank-yous I said a polite, "Good night, Karla," and left.

A day or two later a friend of mine, who saw that I was coming apart at the seams, suggested that I see his psychoanalyst—just for a recommendation. Her name was Ingrid Steiner. I made an appointment, and, after listening to me for a short while, Dr. Steiner called a therapist she knew named Margie . . . ever hear of her?"

Margie smiled.

chapter 11

A TASTE OF FREEDOM

A week after *The White House* closed, I walked into Margie's office
and gave her a cheerful, "Hi."

"What's the matter?" she said.

"What do you mean? . . . All I said was, 'Hi.' "

"What happened?"

I got to the couch and lay down, staring at the ceiling.

"Is there a name for what I've got?"

"Repetition compulsion. Now tell me what happened."

After about a minute of silence, I started to cry. Margie didn't say a
word.

"The Demon came back," I said.

Margie waited.

"I saw a picture of three starving children on the cover of the magazine section of the New York Times. Their stomachs were all bloated. A young doctor was leaning over one of the kids, trying to feed her."

"So? What do you want me to do?"

"Oh, you're just the Angel of Mercy, aren't you? I'm talking about morality."

"Morality is where you draw the line. If you want to hold on to your compulsion, that's your business."

"What the hell are you talking about? You think I like being this way?"

"Maybe."

"Oh, Jesus."

"Are you praying now?"

"Yes! To you! Please—I want you to get rid of my compulsion and get me out of this nonfucking marriage."

"And what will you be doing—playing tennis?"

Long pause. Then Margie said,

"Are you still living with Mary?"

"Yes."

"Not healthy."

"I know it. I can't afford another place."

"Let her go to work."

"Fine! Would you tell her? She thinks it's a husband's responsibility."

"And what's the wife supposed to do?"

"She asked me to please get out of the apartment in the afternoons because she's writing a play now. She's also joined a poetry group in the evenings, with four homosexual men."

"Mister Wilder . . . your marriage stinks."

"Thanks. How much do I owe you for that?"

"Have you seen any other women?"

"No. Not yet. Well . . . just the unhappy nymphomaniac I told you about. But . . ."

"But?"

"I met a little dancer at a party last week. I thought I might ask her out."

"What do you mean by a little dancer?"

"She's four-foot-eleven. She dances on Broadway."

"What's her name?"

"Well, I call her 'Billie' because she reminds me of an adorable Broadway actress I read about who was famous in the twenties."

Margie wrote something in her notepad.

INTERMEZZO

I asked Billie if she'd like to go to dinner with me on Sunday evening—her night off—and she said yes. She knew I was married but "sort of" separated.

We went to a small bistro on the West Side that she knew was open on Sundays, and where she also knew the owner. We shared a coq au vin and a nice bottle of Beaujolais.

Billie wore a very simple, but ever-so-pretty, pink-and-lavender blouse, which went awfully well with her shiny blond hair. She also wore quite a short skirt—with fairly high heels, of course. What she wore looked inexpensive, but still very special, in the way that dancers know how to choose things to wear. It was the best meal I'd had with a woman in a long time.

At the end of the meal, the owner came over and sat down with us, bringing his own glass of whatever he had been drinking. He was a jolly man and told some jokes and told us about a few people he missed very much who still lived in France. From the look in his eyes, I think one of them might have been an old lover. Then he clinked glasses with us and said, "Des souvenirs!" ("To memories!")

After dinner I went to Billie's apartment. We sat on the floor, leaning against her sofa. She played some music—not classical, but mellow forties standards. I kissed her. She kissed back; I wouldn't say passionately, but nicely. Almost politely. I inched my way up the side of her sweater and got close to her breast, which was hard to find because she was almost completely flat chested. My mind started racing. *Seema Clark, Seema Clark, angora sweater, "You're just like all the other boys, aren't you?"* Now here's the thing that knocked me for a loop—she grabbed my hand and plunked it down over her left breast.

"You wanna feel? Then *feel!*"

Well, stop the world, I want to get off. We went into her bedroom, where two tiny Yorkies were sitting on her bed, yapping as we walked in. She took them off the bed, kissed them both, and put them in a little basket on the floor. Then she went into the bathroom to take off her things. I took my clothes off in the bedroom, hiding my nakedness slightly from the two Yorkies. Don't ask me why.

Billie came out, naked, dimmed the lights, and got into bed.

"I don't like anyone touching my privates with their fingers," she announced.

She didn't like using mouths or tongues either, except for kissing.

We made love, and after about twenty minutes—during which time she told me that she knew every inch of Marlon Brando's body—to my great surprise, we did it again. That was a first for me. After another twenty minutes—to my even greater surprise—we did it again.

"Three times! My, my," she said.

She had a strange way of complimenting and belittling me at the same time. However she meant it, I was grateful to her for cutting through my usual malarkey.

Later that night, when I got back to the apartment that I was paying for and "sharing" with Mary, I slipped into my side of the bed and slept without anger in my heart for the first time in many months.

chapter 12

THE KING IS DEAD. LONG LIVE THE KING!

Still no word from Mel.

One Flew Over the Cuckoo's Nest lasted only three months on
Broadway. In March of 1964 The Actors Studio Theater was going
to produce a comic opera called *Dynamite Tonight,* by Arnold
Weinstein, with music by William Bolcom. I was asked to play a
simpleton soldier who loved the movies. Paul Sills, of Second City
fame, had done this project a short while before and was going to
direct, with Barbara Harris as the only star.

When rehearsals began, it became obvious that Paul Sills didn't
want to be doing this. I suppose the prestige of being asked by the famous Lee Strasberg must have influenced his decision to direct *Dynamite* again. But Paul was tired and wanted to get back to Chicago.
He had us do scenes in fast motion, then in slow motion, and then in
every other kind of motion you could think of except "e-motion."

After two weeks Paul Sills was replaced by the author, Arnold Weinstein—a decision that resulted in chaos. To make things worse, we were now giving preview performances each evening, with a small orchestra.

After a few days of humiliation for all of us, Arnold was replaced by Lee Strasberg. Thank God . . . to actually be directed by Lee.

I had several scenes, some of them quite funny, but I had one great scene in which I sang a song called "How I Love the Movies." It had a verse, a chorus, and then a repeat of the chorus.

On the first day that Lee took over, he gave some general notes and then he said, "Gene, we don't need a repeat of that chorus you sing. Once is enough. Otherwise, it stops the show. Tonight, do it without the repeat."

My heart started to race. *Hold on. . . . Hold on.*

"Lee, I think that song is what this whole story is about. This simpleton I play is caught up in a war, and he just wants to be like all the singing and dancing heroes he saw in the movies . . . Fred Astaire, Gene Kelly. . . ."

Lee got agitated. Someone was actually doubting him on artistic matters. The other cast members—who were sitting in the first two or three rows of the theater—listened intently but were afraid to make eye contact with the legend they all worshiped.

"Lee, I don't think there's much point to my character if the audience doesn't see that he—"

Lee turned red.

"CHARACTER? YOU'RE TALKING TO *ME* ABOUT CHARACTER? I'M TELLING YOU IT'S WRONG!"

An emotion I barely recognized came over me; there was no conscious thought. I suddenly screamed at the top of my lungs, "THEN FIRE ME! DO ME A FAVOR AND FIRE ME!"

Lee's face changed from red to blue. He tried to speak, but the words came out hoarse, as if he had laryngitis. "And you're a good actor," he squeaked, "You're a good actor!"

That was the first time I ever had an argument with a director—the only time, I think. (But there have been one or two occasions when I wish I had—when some insecure director took out his frustrations by yelling at an actor or a crew member in front of the whole company.) That night I did the performance as Lee had requested—without the repeat, just singing the verse and one chorus.

The next morning, Mike Nichols took over the direction of *Dynamite Tonight*—at Lee Strasberg's request. After we all said hello to each other, Mike said, "Gene, I saw the show two nights ago—what happened to the repeat of the chorus in your song?"

"Lee thought it was a showstopper," I said.

Mike smiled, with a gentle sense of irony that formed at the ends of his lips. "It's supposed to be a showstopper—that's why they wrote it that way. Tonight, let's put the repeat back, and then let's add a second repeat."

We rehearsed for another week, during which time Mike would say to all of us, "Now what could we do here? What do you think? Anyone have any ideas?" And we all started using our imaginations for the first time in five weeks. *Together,* we reconstructed the entire comic opera. And it was good. Now the audience loved it. I had never seen direction like this.

The opening night went very well. After the curtain came down, Lee came to our communal dressing room and walked up to me. He said, "You were very good tonight." I should have just said, "Thank you, Lee," but the schoolboy in me stupidly answered, "Did you really think so?" He said, "Does it matter what I think?" That was the last time I had any intimate conversation with Lee Strasberg.

METHOD ACTING

When I began studying acting, everyone and his uncle used the word *technique,* but they were usually talking about the mechanics of acting: louder, softer, faster, slower, modulating the tempo . . . things that Strasberg would have said nature takes care of, if you let it. For me, now, technique only means whatever you choose to concentrate on while you're acting. If you choose to concentrate only on the meaning of the lines . . . that's a technique. If you're concentrating on a preconceived idea of how the words should sound as they come out of your mouth, well, that's a technique; not a very good one, perhaps, but many actors have gotten away with it because of their own natural talent, which has nothing to do with technique.

Stanislavsky's system, or "method" as it's now usually referred to, just boils down to finding logical behavior in a situation and then using your own real emotions as you create your part. Strasberg taught many techniques to get to those emotions—I use some of them and I don't use others—but truly *looking* and truly *listening* has always been the heart and soul of any good actor's technique. I don't believe that Spencer Tracy thought much about a lot of technical mumbo-jumbo, but watch him listen to the actors he's working with and you'll see the finest technique you could hope for.

The two most important things I learned at The Actors Studio were: don't use any technique if the situation and the author's words are working for you, by themselves; and, try to stay *in the moment,* which only means that every time you do the same scene, on stage or in front of a camera, if you're relaxed and you're reacting to the other actors *at that moment*—not the way you did it yesterday or fifteen minutes ago—then even though the lines are exactly the same and the staging is exactly the same, the scene will be a little different each time you do it, and it will be alive.

chapter 13

"FREE AT LAST, FREE AT LAST. THANK MARGIE WALLIS, I'M FREE AT LAST."

In 1965, by mutual agreement, Mary and I split up. I said I would finish payments on the lease of our apartment, which had two months to go, and then we would have to settle things with a lawyer. My brain must have had a temporary breakdown because, in order to save money, I hired the same lawyer for both of us.

The lawyer—who should really have been selling used cars—suggested that I pay Mary $50 for every Friday in any given month . . . for the rest of my life, or until she got married again.

I said, "What if I'm unemployed? Where do I get the money?"

He said, "Where you get the money is up to you." (This was my lawyer I was talking to.)

I went home and worked out the following arrangement: I agreed to pay her $50 for every Friday in every month if I was making $25,000 a year or more, but only $25 for every Friday if I was making less than $25,000 a year. This magnificent arrangement was to last for the rest of my life, unless she married. The next day I went to my regular appointment with Margie.

> ME: She doesn't cook or do any housekeeping or take meat out of the freezer or make love . . . and we have no children. I sure pulled a fast one on her, didn't I?
>
> MARGIE: Just don't ever become a lawyer or an accountant. By the way—I think that *little* dancer was good for you.

POEM TO MARY

WHY DO I *NOT* HATE THEE? LET ME COUNT THE WAYS

1. If it hadn't been for you, I wouldn't have been in *Roots*.
2. If I hadn't been in *Roots,* I wouldn't have found my New York agent, Lily Veidt.
3. If I hadn't been in *Roots,* I wouldn't have been in my first television play, *Wingless Victory*.
4. If I hadn't been in *Wingless Victory,* Irene Mayer Selznick wouldn't have seen me and put me in my first Broadway play, *The Complaisant Lover.*
5. I've been very fortunate since the days we both saw that absurd lawyer, and I can afford to pay you this relatively small sum now, and for the rest of my life, even though your taking it is an insult to women, but I don't want to disrupt your life.

I flew to El Paso, where I took a bus to Juarez. As the crowded bus crossed into Mexico, there was a gigantic sign—intended for the Americans, I assume—which advertised: MEXICATESSEN. All of the passengers on the bus were getting divorces and we all stayed at the same hacienda. The next morning I got my divorce. Amen.

MASTER CLASS

I saw Charlie Chaplin in *The Circus* at a Chaplin film festival in New York.

Charlie has just gotten out of prison (one assumes) and is starving. He wanders onto the circus grounds and sees a father carrying his baby over one shoulder. The baby is holding a huge hot dog. The father—whose back is to Charlie—is talking to the man selling the hot dogs. The father looks back at Charlie once or twice.

Charlie makes the sweetest faces at the little boy, and—just when the father isn't looking—he takes a big bite out of the baby's hot dog. The father turns quickly to Charlie, who immediately stops chewing and makes sweet faces at the baby. When the father turns back to the hot dog salesman, Charlie takes another bite of the hot dog. The father turns around again, suspecting something fishy. Charlie stops chewing and makes wonderful googley faces at the baby.

The acting lesson from this film seems so simple, yet it inspired me for the rest of my career: if the thing you're doing is really funny, you don't need to "act funny" while doing it.

SOME LIKE IT BOILING HOT

Still no word from Mel.

In the summer of 1964 I was offered a job in George Bernard Shaw's *The Millionairess,* to be directed by Gene Saks and starring

Carol Channing. It was for a summer tour, but it was supposed to come to Broadway in the fall.

My role in the play was a lawyer. The opening scene takes place in my office, into which the Millionairess (Carol) walks, to tell me what she wants done with her estate . . . fourteen minutes of just Carol Channing and me. (I never told her that I was the young high-school student who asked her if it hurt her throat when she sang and talked in *Gentlemen Prefer Blondes*.)

At the first morning's rehearsal we read through our opening scene. Gene Saks said, "Good! Now let's just walk through this scene, slowly—don't worry about acting—and let's see where our instincts tell us to move."

I sat at my desk. Carol Channing made her entrance. We moved a little bit here and there, only where it seemed logical. When we finished the scene, Gene Saks said, "Good! Very natural. Now let's do that much again and see if we can remember those moves."

We started again. After about forty-five seconds Carol Channing stopped acting, looked out at Gene Saks—who was sitting in the third row of the theater—and said, "Why is he doing that?"

I looked around to see if there was someone else behind me. I was afraid of what it might mean, but I wasn't absolutely sure.

Gene Saks said, "Doing what, Carol?"

"Upstaging me."

I dropped my head. *Oh, God, no . . . a star.*

Gene said, "Carol, that's just the way we rehearsed it."

"It is?"

"Yes, darling. If I thought there was any other reason, I would have stopped it right away."

"Oh."

Hold on to your seats, folks—it's going to be a rough ride.

On our opening night in Louisville, Kentucky, Miss Channing didn't know her lines. She stumbled and fumbled, but somehow we got through it. The cast included real pros . . . Estelle Parsons, John McMartin, David Hurst, and Eugene Roche.

We all came out for curtain calls. After two bows, Miss Channing stepped forward and did an eight-minute nightclub routine while we all stood there like dummies. Why a nightclub routine after doing a Shaw play? I assumed it was because she wanted the audience to love her again, as they always had, and not go away judging her on this performance. I walked off of the stage after about four minutes, and after that night none of us stayed onstage for her nightclub act—which she continued to do after each performance for the remainder of the run.

Gene Saks quit after opening night. We had lunch together the next day. He said he couldn't take it anymore. He wished me luck and said that he and I would work together again, someday. "How come you don't go to Hollywood to get into the movies?" he asked.

I told him that I wouldn't be any good at selling myself. I'd walk into some producer's office, and he'd say, "Hey, I hear you're a funny guy." But I wouldn't be funny, just sitting there, talking to him. "The only way I'll ever get into movies is if some director sees me onstage and wants me for a certain part."

The cast of *The Millionairess* was told that a new director would be joining us at our next engagement, in Westport, Connecticut.

His name was Jerry Epstein, and—we were told—he had been Charlie Chaplin's assistant director.

We were all excited to meet Mr. Epstein when we arrived at the famous Westport Country Playhouse. We got to the playhouse on a Sunday, our day off, in time to rehearse for several hours.

The playhouse was a beautiful old barn, with thin wooden walls and an old screen door on one side of the stage. After some polite

introductions (and a few repetitions of, "Were you really Charlie
Chaplin's assistant director?" "Yes, I was."), Mr. Epstein said, "Let's
run through it once—there are just a few places I'd like to clean up
a little."

Carol and I started the rehearsal. (I'd dropped the "Miss Channing" by this time.) We got to the point in the scene where Carol,
sitting in a chair, says, "I almost respected him for it," and I answer,
"Then why do you want to get rid of him?"

Carol said her line. I paused for a moment. Carol burst out
with, "Just shoot that line right in there!"

Hold on, Gene. . . . Hold on. . . .

"Do you mean . . . take out any pause?" I asked.

"Yes! Just shoot that line right in there!"

I walked down the three steps leading to the orchestra floor
and walked up the aisle to the third row, where Jerry Epstein was
sitting.

"Does the director want me to 'just shoot that line right in
there'?"

After a mournful sigh, he said, "Come on, Gene. . . ."

"I'm asking you a question: does the director of this play want
me to just shoot that line right in there?"

He got a sick look on his face. "Yes . . . I do."

I walked back onto the stage, as calmly as I could, and asked
Carol to give me my cue again. "I almost respected him for it," she
said.

Without a millisecond of a pause, I leaned over and shouted
into her ear so loudly that the walls of the old barn started shaking, "THEN WHY DO YOU WANT TO GET RID OF HIM?"

There was a stunned silence from everyone. Then Carol jumped
up and, in a very hoarse voice, said, "Who opened the door?"

Jerry Epstein jumped out of his seat.

"What, Carol? What's the matter?"

"My allergies," she said. "Somebody must have opened a door." She ran off the stage, passing the screen door, which was filled with holes, and then she scampered downstairs to her dressing room. It was my first introduction to "hysterical laryngitis." When she came back onstage five minutes later, her voice had returned, and she never mentioned the screaming or the pause again.

The play opened the next night, and Carol still didn't know her lines. When actors can't remember their lines, it's called "going up," or "taking the elevator." At one point in the third act, Carol went up higher than a kite. The audience was aware of it. Carol looked at me.

"What's your problem, mister?"

I said, "I don't have the problem, dear—you're the one who has the problem."

The audience burst into applause.

When the curtain came down, Estelle Parsons told Carol, "Either you know your lines by tomorrow night, or I'm not going onstage." I imagine that Carol's husband was up with her till the wee hours. The following evening Carol knew her lines—word perfect.

Several weeks later, when we gave the final performance of the play in Nyack, New York, I finished my last scene and didn't wait for the curtain call to change into my street clothes. We all knew that this show was never going to Broadway, and I just wanted to get out of that theater as quickly as I could, hopefully without saying good-bye. I made for the stage door, but just before I reached it, I heard, "Gene—would you come here for a minute?"

Her dressing room door was open. Carol was sitting in her panties and bra, with a little towel over her lap. She wasn't wearing her wig. I walked over to her and stood in the open doorway.

"I know I've been difficult to work with," she said. "I want to thank you for putting up with me. It must have been terribly annoying for all of you."

I assumed she meant the "nightclub act" after each curtain call, or perhaps the fact that her husband started every applause for her, matinée and evening. There was something vulnerable in the way she looked at me that I hadn't seen before.

"I need it," she said.

My heart sank. I gave her a smile and a gentle nod good-bye as all the bitterness drained out of me. I thought she expressed more awareness of what had happened that summer than I would have thought she was capable of.

"Thank you, Carol. Good night."

MARGIE: What's with this screaming-at-a-woman business? You never screamed at a woman before?

ME: Once a year. I screamed at my mother when I couldn't hold it in anymore.

MARGIE: How did it feel?

ME: Terrible. I couldn't stop crying. I don't want you to think that I don't ever get angry, but letting the anger at Carol burst out of me that way—no thinking, just the rage pouring out—that was new. My screaming wasn't such a big deal—it was kind of funny in a way, and it makes a good story. I think the big deal was that I did it in front of all those people.

Margie waited for me to catch up with where I think she wanted me to go.

MARGIE: Tell me.

ME: When I was a kid, my mom and dad took me to a restaurant that specialized in barbecued spareribs and delicious ice cream sodas. On the front of the menu, it said, "Pig on the Cob." My dad and I had the spareribs; my mother had an orange ice cream soda. In between bites of his pig on the cob—which my father, by some strange Jewish logic, assumed meant "ribs of beef"—he said, "Annette wanted me to buy that chair from her for $150, and I told her, 'Personally, I think it's a piece of junk, but my wife wants it, so, okay, I'll give you $50 for it.'" He said it in the cutest way—as if he were telling a joke.

My mother turned red and said, "Annette introduced us! We wouldn't be married if it hadn't been for Annette!"

"What'd I say? Annette didn't mind. She even laughed when I said it."

"I'm not cheap!"

"Of course you're not cheap. Who said anything about cheap? All I said was—"

"I KNOW WHAT YOU SAID! If we didn't have a penny to our name, I still wouldn't be cheap! Annette's going to think that we're cheap."

The people at the table next to us turned to watch. My father stopped eating.

"Jeanne—what'd I say? It was nothing. I was just making a little joke."

My mother stood up and started hollering. "I KNOW WHAT YOU SAID! DON'T KEEP SAYING IT WAS NOTHING. . . . IT WASN'T A JOKE!"

Now all the people in the restaurant turned to look at us. My father was baffled.

"Jeanne, come on now, honey—don't get so excited or you're going to get sick. All I said to her was—"

"ALL YOU SAID TO HER WAS THAT WE'RE TOO CHEAP AND WE CAN'T AFFORD TO BUY A CHAIR."

I put my chin on my chest. I was afraid to look at any of the people who were watching us. My lips kept moving without making sounds: *Please stop, please stop, everyone's watching.* . . . But at the same time I was thinking, *Good for you, Mama, good for you. What courage—to scream in front of the whole restaurant. Poor Daddy. Good for you, Mama.*

After a long pause, Margie said, "Time's up, Gene. See you Wednesday."

MY FIRST LOVE

I was asked by Mike Nichols to "stand by" for Alan Arkin and Eli Wallach in Murray Schisgal's play *Luv,* which Mike was going to direct in the fall. "Stand by" is a polite way of saying "understudy," with one great difference: if you're a stand by, you don't have to go to the theater each night—you just call in half an hour before curtain to see if the actor you're standing by for has arrived. Mike said, "You'll turn me down, but I'm going to ask you anyway. You might find it better than acting in some junk." That fall I was offered other jobs, but they were all junk. So I decided to stand by until something worthwhile came along.

One afternoon, Corinne asked if I'd like to come to dinner. She had invited her former college roommate, Mary Jo, and thought maybe I'd like to join them. "You remember Mary Jo, don't you?" (Mary Jo, whose "original lips" I dreamed of kissing long after I said good-bye to her in Iowa City, thirteen years ago.) I said, "Sure, I'd like to join you."

Everyone close to Mary Jo just called her Jo. She had married, disastrously, had a five-and-a-half-year-old daughter by that marriage, and left her husband before the baby was born. Jo looked almost the same as she did when we first met. Her little daughter, Katie, was wild—adorable and wild. I made her laugh during dinner and by the end of the evening I knew that she liked me.

After dinner I walked Jo and Katie to their apartment building, which, by some curious happenstance, was only six blocks away from my new one-room apartment on Seventy-third Street, just off of Madison Avenue (rent-controlled for $214.00 per month). The next day I called Jo and asked her for a date. We went to see Sidney Poitier in *A Patch of Blue*. During the movie I put my arm around her shoulders. She responded warmly. I took her home and kissed her good night. It was a beautiful kiss.

SALESMAN REVISITED

Alex Segal—the man who had directed me in *One Flew Over the Cuckoo's Nest*—called and asked if I would come over to David Susskind's office. When I got there, he offered me the part of Bernard in a two-hour CBS television presentation of *Death of a Salesman,* starring Lee J. Cobb and Mildred Dunnock. It felt as if life was playing a game with me.

I got a four-week leave of absence from my job with *Luv* and flew to Los Angeles. I stayed at the Montecito Hotel, sometimes referred to as the Actors' Hotel, because you could get a living room/bedroom, plus kitchenette, for eighty-five dollars a month. We rehearsed for three weeks in a huge building on Beverly Boulevard, next to CBS Television City.

I had rented a little Volkswagen so I could drive to and from rehearsals. I didn't know Los Angeles very well, but the assistant director gave me a very simple route to take from my hotel to the rehearsal hall.

One day, after rehearsal, I thought I knew my way well enough to try a slightly different route back to the hotel. I had been driving for about five minutes when suddenly my whole body got clammy. I felt as if all the blood had drained out of my face. My arms were warm, but my forehead was cold. I thought I'd better pull over before I had an accident. I was on Melrose Avenue and Wilcox. When I looked up, I saw the Black/Foxe Military Institute drill field right in front of me. I was staring at the same field that I had marched on, twice a day, just before being beaten up each night. My sense memory knew what my brain didn't.

After three weeks of rehearsal we taped *Death of a Salesman* in four days. I never told Lee J. Cobb how my life had changed after I saw him on Broadway in this same play, when I was sixteen years old. It seems stupid now—not to have told him—but I was afraid it would sound mushy.

Mildred Dunnock, however, became my new best friend—during rehearsals and the taping—always giving me encouragement and a smile when I finished a scene. And when I needed advice, I turned to Mildred.

On our last day, after we finished taping, she asked if I'd like to have dinner with her. I said I would like that very much, so long as I was paying. There was a favorite restaurant she used to go to when she worked in Los Angeles, called Don the Beachcomber. She introduced me to Mai Tais.

When I got back to New York, I was asked to take over Alan Arkin's role in *Luv* and play it until it closed, sixth months later. I was on Broadway for the fifth time. I also started seeing Mary Jo regularly. The Demon had not left his calling card for months now; I felt almost impregnable. I was also in love, for the first time.

chapter 14

"SORRY I CAUGHT YOU WITH THE OLD LADY."

It had now been three years since I heard from Mel Brooks. In all that time I never got a phone call from him, or a letter, or a telegram. I had given up hopes of being Leo Bloom in *Springtime for Hitler*.

I was taking off my makeup one day, after a matinée performance of *Luv*, when someone knocked on my dressing room door. I opened the door and there was Mel, standing in the hallway, with a tall gentleman standing behind him.

"Mel!" I said, in a slight state of shock.

"You don't think I forgot, do you?" He said it very seriously.

Then he introduced me to the tall gentleman with him, Sydney Glazier, who was going to produce *Springtime for Hitler*. Mel started talking as if he were just continuing a conversation from yesterday.

"Now listen—you know I love you, but Zero Mostel is going to play Bialystock, and I can't just spring you on him because he's got approval of anyone who plays Leo, so you've got to do a reading with him, just so he can see for himself how good you are."

The morning of the reading I went to my regular appointment with Margie, dressed in a "character coat" I had borrowed from the wardrobe rack at *Luv.*

"What's the matter?" Margie asked.

"If I don't get this part, I'll just be a good featured—maybe supporting actor—for the rest of my life."

"Don't you think you're exaggerating a little, Gene?"

"Margie, you know more about psychology than I ever will . . . but I know more about show business than you do."

A few hours later I knocked on Sidney Glazier's office door. It was 11:30 A.M. Mel opened the door and gave me a hug—I could see Zero Mostel in the background—and then Mel pulled me into the office.

"Gene . . . this is Z. Z . . . this is Gene."

This huge, round, fantasy of a man came waltzing towards me. My heart was pounding so loud I thought he'd hear it. I stuck out my hand, politely, to shake his, but instead of shaking my hand Zero pulled me into his body and gave me a giant kiss, on the lips. All nervousness floated away. (I think Zero did it for that reason.) I gave a good reading and was cast in *Springtime for Hitler.*

A BELATED THANK-YOU NOTE TO
JEROME ROBBINS

Dear Jerry:

When we worked together it was the best of times and the worst of times. But I'm more grateful to you now than I ever could have conceived I would be. I'll tell you why:

1. If you hadn't miscast me in Mother Courage, I wouldn't have met Anne Bancroft.
2. If I hadn't met Anne Bancroft, I wouldn't have met Mel Brooks.
3. If I hadn't met Mel Brooks, I would probably be a patient in some neuropsychiatric hospital today, looking through the bars of a physical therapy window as I made wallets.

MY FIRST MOVIE

It was March. Filming on *Springtime for Hitler* was to begin in May, but in the meantime I was offered a small part in a movie called *Bonnie and Clyde,* starring Warren Beatty and to be directed by Arthur Penn. The company was already filming in Texas. I got a one-week leave of absence from *Luv.* My understudy took over for me.

I arrived in Dallas on a Monday afternoon and was driven forty miles to the smallish hotel where everyone (except the stars) was staying. On Tuesday morning I went to the set—which was just someone's big outdoor porch. Arthur Penn introduced me to the pretty young woman who would be playing my fiancée. Her name was Evan Evans.

"Evan, this is Gene—Gene, this is Evan."

We said hello and shook hands. Then Arthur said, "All right, why don't we run through this first scene—just lightly—while the camera is setting up?"

The first scene started with Evan and me kissing on her porch, until I notice that my car is being stolen. We started our rehearsal locked in a big embrace, as we kissed, and after a few moments Arthur said, "Now they're stealing your car, Gene." I jumped up and said my line—something like, "Hey, that's my car!" Arthur said, "Good! All right—let's try one."

Evan and I started kissing, the camera started rolling, and the assistant director yelled, "CAR!" I jumped up and said, "Hey, that's my car!" Arthur said, "Cut! Very good! Let's do one more, and then we'll move on."

And that was my introduction to movie acting. Fun! A little strange, to start kissing someone you'd just met two minutes earlier . . . but it was fun.

Three weeks later I flew to Los Angeles to do the interiors of my scenes in *Bonnie and Clyde*. We were on a Warner Bros. sound stage. My first scene began with Evan and me sitting in the back of her car, supposedly chasing the Barrow Gang. I waited for Arthur Penn to call, "Action." Arthur was sitting alongside the camera— out of frame, of course—but not more than five or six feet away from me. As soon as I heard him say, "Action," I started to act. Sounds sensible, doesn't it? But Arthur immediately called out to the camera operator, "Keep rolling," and then he gave me my first revelation of what it means to be an "actor's director." While the camera was rolling, he said, "Gene, just because I say 'Action,' doesn't mean you have to start acting—it just means that *we're* ready. I could see you had something cooking inside, but you weren't ready to act yet. Film is cheap. Keep working on whatever you're working on and start acting when you're ready."

The scene went very well.

When we took a break, the assistant director came up to me and said, "Don't get used to what just happened—you're not going to find many directors who work like Arthur."

In the next scene I'm riding in the back of a car with the Barrow Gang. Near the end of the scene Gene Hackman tells me a joke. Arthur Penn asked us to rehearse the scene, very lightly, before filming it. When we got to the joke I asked Gene not to tell me the punch line until the cameras were rolling, because I didn't want to feel obligated to fake my laughter when the time came. We started the scene, which was going very well, and then Gene told me the joke. Well, the joke was so dumb that when it came to the punch line—"Whatever you do, don't sell that cow!"—I laughed until there were tears in my eyes, because I couldn't believe how dumb this silly joke was that I had been waiting to hear. (From an acting point of view, not having heard the joke before had helped me a great deal.) We did the scene several times, and I laughed harder each time—mostly, I think, because Gene Hackman was so enthusiastic each time he told me this stupid joke.

When filming was over, Arthur Penn told me that he had never envisioned the part being played the way I did it. I asked him what he meant, and he said he never imagined its being funny. Then I asked him why he thought of me for the part.

"I saw you on Broadway and thought you'd be right for the part."

A few months later I asked Warren Beatty the same question. He said, "I saw you on Broadway and thought you'd be right for the part."

Maybe I'm exaggerating—to the extent that they didn't use the exact same words—but who cares? They both said that I was in a movie because they had seen me onstage, which was just what I told Gene Saks would happen, in Louisville, Kentucky, when he quit directing The Millionairess.

chapter 15

SECOND MOVEMENT

SPRINGTIME FOR HITLER

In May of 1967 I went to my first press luncheon. It was on the afternoon before filming was going to start on *Springtime for Hitler*. Everyone had a place card. Mine was not at the main table, which had place cards for Mel Brooks, Joe Levine (the man who had put up half the budget), Sidney Glazier, Zero Mostel, and Dick Shawn. Zero examined all the place cards; then he picked up Dick Shawn's card and my card and very deftly, like a ballet dancer, swapped them. I was now sitting next to Zero.

When dessert was being served, I got up and excused myself. Mel asked where I was going, I told him that I had a doctor's appointment that I couldn't miss. The truth was that I didn't want to miss signing up for my last unemployment check. (It was up to fifty-five dollars a week by that time.)

Katie had never seen her biological father. He had wined and dined Mary Jo and led her to believe that he was a big shot in the investment business. When Jo became pregnant with Katie, she found out that her husband was not only a liar, but was also broke and a drunkard. She told him that he was not going to be the father to her child. So she walked out after three months of marriage and raised Katie on her own.

I started having dinner with Jo and Katie two or three nights a week. Before dinner was ready, I would perform "circus tricks" with Katie. I would lie down on the floor, with my knees pointed up, and Katie would try to stand on my knees while I held her hands. It always made her laugh—especially when she would start to fall and I would catch her. Then the three of us would sit down to eat.

After dinner I would kiss Katie good night, and Jo would put her to bed. When Jo came out of the bedroom, she'd lower the lights in the living room, and we would lie down together on her couch, fully clothed. Then the habit started: after about twenty minutes Katie would open her bedroom door with a devilish grin on her face and say, "Hi, Daddy."

"DYING IS EASY. COMEDY IS HARD."

Comedy is hard—if you're not a comic actor. And drama is hard if you're not a dramatic actor. Some actors are blessed with the talent to be good in both—Spencer Tracy and Cary Grant, for example. I wish I were blessed that way, but I'll never be as good in drama as I am in comedy. Still, good acting is good acting. As Bette Davis told Paul Henreid at the end of the film *Now Voyager*, "We have the stars, Jerry—why ask for the moon?"

Zero Mostel had a car and driver assigned to him when filming for *Springtime for Hitler* began. I was surprised when he announced that he would pick me up each morning and that we could travel to work together.

Joe Levine—the man who put up half the budget and was going to distribute the film—went to a screening room with Mel and saw the first eleven minutes of the dailies. After he saw them, he said, "I don't know what the hell that Wilder guy is doing. I got twenty-five thousand dollars for you to get yourself another actor."

Mel calmed him down and talked him out of having me fired. (I was only getting ten thousand dollars.) Mel didn't tell me about this incident until a few days later.

Toward the end of the next day, we were about to rehearse my big "hysterical" scene for the next day's filming. I was anxious to see how Zero and I would play it together. Mel said, "Go!"—he never said, "Action," like every other director—and I gave it my all. When the scene was over, the whole crew laughed and applauded. I was worn out and a little hoarse, but I could see that it was going to work when we filmed it the next morning.

Mel looked a little dazed. "What do you mean, 'tomorrow'? We're filming it today! Right now! We've got just enough time."

"Oh, Mel—oh, my God! I thought we were just rehearsing. Wait a minute. . . . Wait a minute. . . ."

An image flashed into my mind. I remembered fencing for the All School Championship at the Bristol Old Vic. I was sweating and felt depleted of all my energy. My fencing master called out, "Jerry, grab a handful of that raw sugar."

I said, "Mel—get me some Hershey bars."

"Hershey bars??"

"Yes, Hershey bars!"

"With or without nuts?"

"It doesn't matter! Just get me—no, wait! *Without nuts*—the nuts might get caught in my throat in the middle of the scene."

Somebody ran out and got some Hershey bars. I ate two of them, had a drink of water, and said, "Ready!"

I had given the scene some prior thought, of course, but only just enough to decide what would get my "motor" going: *This giant hulk of a man—not the character called Bialystock, but Zero Mostel, the actual actor standing in front of me, who grabbed hold of me in Sidney Glazer's office and kissed me,* on the lips—*is now making all these strange gestures and keeps trying to get me down on the floor and pounce on me....*

The scene went very well.

There was another scene that might illuminate more of the way I work. The character I played in the film was called Leo Bloom, and he always carried a blue security blanket with him everywhere he went. Zero Mostel grabbed my little piece of blue blanket, and I nearly went *crazy* until he gave it back. At the time we were filming *Springtime for Hitler,* I had a little dog named Julie. I had made the saddest mistake when I first got her, a year earlier. I took her to Central Park and kept throwing a ball for her to chase. She loved the game, as most dogs do, but one time I threw the ball too hard and too far, and it rolled into one of those water ponds that are emptied in the winter. Julie ran after the ball and then dove into the cement pond and disappeared. I ran to get her, and when I reached the pond, I saw Julie limping on the cold cement as she tried to walk towards me. Now, a year later, when I took out my blue blanket and rubbed it against my cheek, I did a sense memory: I imagined that it was Julie I was holding—not a blue blanket—and I was rubbing my cheek against her curly fur, feeling it and smelling it. And then Zero Motel grabbed her out of my arms and was going to throw her away . . . and I went crazy.

We were at the Lincoln Center fountain on the last day of filming, waiting for the sun to go down. I was sad that the film was ending, of course, but also very happy. I wasn't broke; I was in love—for the first time in my life—and I knew that I had been part of a unique film, working with the two most unusual people I had ever met. The outrageousness—the complete audacity—of Zero and Mel remains with me. Once in a while, when I'm confronted by some pompous authority figure who thinks that his job outranks any artistic concerns, I think of Zero and how he might handle the situation: let out a loud fart and then say, "Oops, I beg your pardon. . . . now what was it you were saying?"

When the sun finally went down, the cameras started rolling, and I started running around the edge of the Lincoln Center fountain, shouting for all I was worth, "I want everything I've ever seen in the movies!" And the fountain was turned on, in the film and in my life.

"HI, DADDY!"

July 1967

MARGIE: You want to get married?

ME: Yes.

MARGIE: And you're sure?

ME: I know that I love her.

MARGIE: I didn't ask you that. I know you love her. I'm asking if you're sure you want to get married.

ME: I can't go on any longer letting that little girl call me "Daddy." It makes me feel good, but it hurts, too, because I'm not her daddy and she's never had a daddy. . . .

Pause.

MARGIE: Where are you?

ME: I'm right here—I didn't go away.

MARGIE: What are you thinking?

ME: If Jo and I get married—do you think it will last?

MARGIE: So long as she adores you.

"LOVE AND MARRIAGE
GO TOGETHER LIKE A HORSE AND CARRIAGE."

Katie's biological father showed up one day at Jo's apartment. Jo asked him what the hell he was doing there, and he answered that he was hoping to see his daughter, just for a few minutes. Jo said something like, "You wait seven years, and now you want to see her?" She kicked him out and told me later how grateful she was that Katie hadn't answered the door.

Springtime for Hitler finished filming in June. I flew with Jo to El Paso, Texas, and took the bus to Juarez, passing the same gigantic sign, MEXICATESSEN, as we crossed into Mexico. Jo got her divorce the next morning.

We were married in October. Katie was seven years old. I found a small, but beautiful, garden apartment on Eightieth Street, between Park Avenue and Madison Avenue, for $480 a month. (Four-hundred-eighty?? Yes!)

There was a single tree in the middle of our small garden. Katie and I went out there on the day we moved into our new home. I carved a heart shape in the bark with a small paring knife, and in the middle of the heart, I carved:

G W

LOVES

K W

Katie wrote me a little note that night:

I love gene. he is thin. he is handsome.

I wanted to adopt Katie as soon as possible, but there was a New York State law that required a six-month waiting period. We were a happy family. I loved it when Katie bounced into bed with Jo and me, just for a little while before going to her own bed, so that we could all watch *Creature Features*—old black-and-white monster movies that Katie was too frightened to watch alone. But the scary parts made her laugh when we all watched together. After six months we went to a courthouse in lower Manhattan.

THE JUDGE: Now Katie, do you want to be adopted?

KATIE: I don't know.

("Oh, my God—now what?")

THE JUDGE: Well, Katie—you know that your mommy and Gene are married, and they love you, and they both want you to be very happy. But I need to know if you really want to be adopted.

KATIE: (with a devilish smile): . . . I don't know.

The judge asked Jo and me to leave the room. While we waited in the courtroom, I tried to figure out what could possibly have gone wrong. After only two minutes we were asked to come back into the judge's office. As we walked in, the judge shook my hand and said, "Congratulations. You're a father."

After Jo and Katie left the office, I waited behind to ask the judge if he would tell me what happened. He said, "I just asked Katie if she wanted you to be her daddy . . . and she said yes."

———

the Jews in the Midwest, so Mel changed the title to *The Producers*. One week before the film opened, Joe got a call from Peter Sellers in the middle of the night. He told Joe that he had just seen the funniest comedy in the last twenty years and asked him why on earth he had changed the title. The next day Joe called Mel Brooks.

"You want to change it back?"

"Are you crazy?" Mel asked. "I fought for *Springtime for Hitler*. You said no. We're opening in Philadelphia next week! All the advertising is done! All the posters are up! And *now* you want to change it back??"

The Producers opened in November.

After I was nominated for an Academy Award for playing Leo Bloom, I was walking through the halls of Joe Levine's empire—called Embassy Pictures—and on my way to the publicity department I heard Joe holler from his office, "YOU'RE A GREAT ACTOR, GENE WILDER!"

Thanks, Joe . . . *for not insisting that Mel fire me.*

chapter 16

BLACK IS MY FAVORITE COLOR.

MARGIE: Tell me.

ME: This is going to sound crazy—well, I guess I'm in the right
place—but all my life I've consciously avoided spitting, on the
sidewalk or street if there was a black person near me.

MARGIE: Why?

ME: Because I didn't want them to think I was spitting at them.

MARGIE: Why would they think that?

ME: I don't know. I just didn't want to take the chance of offending
a black person.

MARGIE: Why?

ME: Probably because my dad once hired a black man named Joe.
When I was three years old, my father had started experiment-

ing with resin in the basement of our apartment building, melt-
ing it down to liquid and then pouring it into shot glasses and
miniature beer glasses. When the resin hardened, it looked like
real whiskey and beer, and he'd sell the glasses a dozen at a
time—until they threw us out of our apartment building because of the stink. When I was four, my dad rented a tiny store
and hired Joe to help him. Joe used to pick me up and carry me
around the store on his shoulders. When the war broke out, he
was drafted, and if any of the kids in my neighborhood ever
started in with the usual, "My dad could beat up your dad," I'd
say, "Well, Joe could beat up your dad and your brothers and
your uncles and anyone else you know."

MARGIE: Who did you spit on?

ME: I was walking home from the grocery store today and I felt a
bug or a mosquito or something fly into my throat, and I spit it
out just as an elderly black woman was about to pass me on the
sidewalk. She thought I was spitting at her, so she spat back and
said, "I can spit at you, too. How do *you* like it?"

MARGIE: And that set off your compulsion?

ME: No. No compulsion. It just struck me how ironic it was. I let
my spitting guard down one time in all these years, and I hurt
some old black lady. It made me sad.

MARGIE: And if it had been some old white lady, what would you
have said?

ME: I would have just said, "Excuse me."

James Brooks said that he had written a character just for me after
he saw *The Producers.* He wanted me to act in a movie for television called *Thursday's Game,* with Bob Newhart as my partner in a
clothing business, Ellen Burstyn as my wife, Cloris Leachman as
Bob's wife, Valerie Harper as my secretary, Norman Fell as my em-

ployer, Nancy Walker as my unemployment counselor, and Rob Reiner as my agent. I said yes.

The biggest problem I had during the seven weeks of filming was trying not to break up laughing when I was acting in a scene with Bob Newhart. It was a constant problem. After the second or third time that Bob and I broke up laughing in the middle of one particular scene, the director—instead of letting the laughter play itself out—made us feel like we were naughty third-grade children, and when he did that, I always felt like saying, "Well, Bob started it!" But of course Bob would probably have said, "Well, Gene started it," so I kept my mouth shut.

On the last day of filming *Thursday's Game,* we were outside in downtown Los Angeles, which was supposed to be New York. We even had a fake Yellow Cab with fake New York license plates. We finished filming at midnight, and the producer sent Bob and me home in the same fake Yellow Cab, along with a pile of our own clothing that we had loaned to the production. A Teamster driver drove us.

When we got to Bob's home in Beverly Hills, we both got out of the cab, carrying a bundle of Bob's clothes. We started walking toward the front door, and then a police car drove up. One of the cops yelled, "HOLD IT RIGHT THERE!"

Bob said, "Officer—"

"SHUT UP AND MOVE BACK TO THE CAB!"

Bob said, "Well, it's not really a cab, Officer, it's—"

"SHUT UP AND DROP THOSE CLOTHES."

We started laughing.

"THINK IT'S FUNNY? FACE THE CAB, BOTH OF YOU, AND PUT YOUR HANDS ON THE ROOF."

Now we were scared. We dropped the clothes, faced the cab, and put our hands on the roof.

"Officer, we're not—we're not stealing these clothes. These are *my* clothes. You see—we're both actors. This is Gene Wilder, here, and I'm Bob Newhart, and Gene was just helping me get my clothes into my house."

"WHERE'D YOU STEAL THE CAB FROM?"

I bit my cheeks so I wouldn't laugh. Bob said, "Uh, no Officer. That's not a cab."

"SHUT YOUR MOUTH AND SPREAD YOUR LEGS APART!"

Now we both broke up and couldn't stop laughing.

"THINK IT'S FUNNY?"

Bob tried to sound logical. "No, Officer—no, sir, not at all. It's just that—this cab is not really a cab. . . . It's a fake cab."

"IT'S GOT NEW YORK LICENSE PLATES. DID YOU STEAL THOSE TOO?"

"No, sir. . . . Those are . . . those are fake license plates."

The other policeman, who was with the bulldog who was doing all the talking, whispered something into the bulldog's ear.

"YOU'RE ACTORS, HUH?"

We both said, "Yes, sir," as sweetly as we could.

"ALL RIGHT, YOU CAN DROP YOUR HANDS."

We both said, "Thank you, Officer," at the same time.

As the bulldog got back into his police car, he yelled out, "AND DON'T LET THIS HAPPEN AGAIN!"

ALL THAT GLITTERS IS NOT GOLD

In 1967, when I visited Mel in a recording studio as he was putting music into *Springtime for Hitler,* I was told that there was a phone call for me from Mike Nichols. *Bonnie and Clyde* hadn't opened yet, but Arthur Penn showed Mike the outtakes of my scenes from *Bonnie and Clyde.*

Mike said, "I'm going to do *Catch-22*. Promise me you'll be in it." I said, "Mike, I'd rather work with you than anyone, but I never read *Catch-22*. I don't know it at all."

"Get it! Read it! The part is Milo Minderbinder. We're filming in Mexico. Promise me you'll be in the movie."

"If I'm right for the part, I promise you I'll be in the movie."

That night I read the book and loved it. I could see why Mike wanted me for Milo Minderbinder—someone who's doing the most horrible things during World War II but thinks that he's doing good for everyone.

A few days later I got a call to meet with Norman Lear at his office in New York. When I got there, he offered me the leading role in a big film he was producing called *Start the Revolution Without Me*—a comedy that took place during the French Revolution. His partner, Bud Yorkin, would be directing. I would play twins—a peasant and an aristocrat. It was going to be filmed in Czechoslovakia that summer. The script arrived the next day, and I loved it.

The film script for *Catch-22* arrived by messenger a few days later. I didn't have to make a choice. The irony of Milo Minderbinder had not made it into the script, except for a few token sentences. It was just about all the horrible things that Milo was doing—without his crazy rationale for why he was doing them. I felt that there was nothing for me to act. I accepted *Start the Revolution Without Me*.

A few weeks later, Russia invaded Czechoslovakia, and our location was changed to Paris.

ALL THIS AND PARIS TOO

In June, Jo, Katie, and I flew to London, where I got fitted for costumes and wigs, and then a week later we flew to Paris. This was an actor's dream—something you might fantasize about, knowing it will never happen. But it *did* happen! Wigs, costumes, Paris! Donald Sutherland was cast in the other leading role, and he was also playing twins. Two actors in four parts. This would be fun.

I had never heard of "French hours" before, but what a wonderful idea it is. Since so many French actors who work in films during the day also work onstage at night, filming in France doesn't begin until noon. But there's a terrible trap involved. The production company lays out an enormous lunch at 11:00 A.M. For the crew that's fine, but it's deadly for the poor American actor who, after lunch, has to act straight through until 7:00 P.M. At my first lunch there weren't any tuna salad sandwiches; all these cheapskates served was appetizer, main course, white wine, red wine, cheese, fruit, and dessert. After the first lunch I learned to say, "No, *merci.*"

Orson Welles was playing the Narrator in *Start the Revolution Without Me,* and I wanted to meet him. He only had two filming days, and I thought it would be more polite if I waited until the second day to say hello. On the second day, at about three in the afternoon, I got to the chateau where they were filming; Orson Welles was gone. I asked Bud Yorkin what happened.

"Well," Bud said, "we'd start a scene, and after a little while Orson would call 'Cut!' He'd look at me and say, 'Now, you don't honestly want any more of that shot, do you, Bud? Surely you'll be cutting to the twins at that point.' And I'd say, 'Yes . . . well . . . yes, I suppose so.' Then we'd be in the middle of the next scene, and he'd yell, 'Cut!' and he'd say, 'Now surely you've got to cut there, Bud—it wouldn't make any sense if you didn't cut to the mob at that point.' So we finished shooting all of his sequences an hour ago."

It rained almost every day that summer. As much as I loved Paris, it was difficult for Katie. The rain made for beautiful photography, but for an eight year old to go swimming or play outside was nearly impossible. There would be the odd day of sunshine, but mostly there was rain.

Food also was a problem for Katie. We were in the gastronomic capital of the world, and all she wanted to eat was pizza or a plain broiled steak. I didn't blame her. What's a great sauce to an eight-year-old? We found a place called the American Restaurant not far from where we lived, so when we didn't eat in our apartment, we went to the American Restaurant for steak, baked potatoes, and ice cream. Jo found a lovely baby-sitter—a young French girl named Georgina who spoke English perfectly. If Jo and I wanted to go out to a restaurant, Georgina would take Katie to the Champs Elysées, to a place called Pizza Pino, and that made Katie happy.

"HELLO, I MUST BE GOING."

September came, and Jo had to leave so that Katie could go back to school in New York. We all kissed good-bye. I gave up the apartment we had all lived in and moved to a small hotel just off the Champs Elysées. For me, living alone is nice . . . for about a day.

On my first evening alone I was eating at a popular bistro, just finishing my dinner as I read the *International Herald Tribune,* when in walked Orson Welles. He was accompanied by three other people, who looked like they were all working together on a film. Why did I feel so embarrassed at the thought that Orson Welles might happen to see me? I have no idea. I suppose because he was a great star, and I didn't want to intrude on his privacy. Or perhaps it was out of my own ego, afraid that the director of *Citizen Kane* wouldn't know me from Adam, and then I would have to remind him that I was the fellow who had the lead in the film he worked on for two days last month.

I quickly paid my check, covered my face with my *Herald Tribune,* stooped over—like Groucho Marx—and duck-walked across the floor as quickly as I could. Just as I reached the door, I heard, "OH, MR. WILDER!"

I turned and saw Orson Welles standing beside his table, beckoning to me to come over. When I got there, he introduced me to his friends, and then said, "I hope I didn't disturb you. I just wanted you to know what a pleasure it is to meet you, Mr. Wilder. I'm a great admirer of yours. Thank you for coming over." In the taxi on my way back to the hotel, I wondered if I could truly absorb this lesson in generosity that was unfettered by ego.

Towards the end of October we were filming on a quay along the river Seine. It was one of the last scenes to be done before we all said good-bye.

I was sitting alone at the water's edge, watching actresses dressed as great ladies get in and out of 1789 carriages, with the fringe of their white petticoats showing underneath their long dresses. Tall men dressed as aristocrats, in beautiful blue satin costumes, rehearsed their sword fights on the steps of the quay. Ducks, geese, and pigs were being loaded onto 1789 barges—all in preparation for the next shot.

I sat watching all these things, and a deep sadness came over me. Nothing to do with the Demon—it had to do with real life. Well, that's a silly thing to say, because nothing I had been seeing or doing for the past three months was real; it was a movie. It was all remote from everyday experience. Even the real cobblestoned streets in Paris and the old buildings and houses that were constructed with curves and rounded moldings were all fantastical and very romantic. At first I thought I was sad at the thought of going back to the straight lines and glass rectangles of New York; then I realized that I was actually afraid of going back to Jo and Katie, which made no sense to me at the time.

On the plane ride home I began writing my first screenplay, which I called *Hesitation Waltz*. It was never produced.

chapter 17

"I HAVE A REASON—I JUST DON'T KNOW WHAT IT IS."

When I got back to New York, we had a warm family reunion, but during the next several months little troubles started popping up, like buds in spring. Emily Dickinson wrote, "The heart wants what it wants, when it wants it, or else it doesn't care." It was certainly what Katie felt, and she was just eight years old.

I was holding Katie's hand one day as we were walking along the sidewalk on our way to the butcher, and she said that she wanted me to buy her some strange mechanical contraption that she saw in the stationery shop next to the butcher. I thought the thing she wanted was a little bizarre, apart from being fairly expensive.

"Why do you want that crazy thing?" I asked.

"I just want it."

"I know you want it—I'm not saying I won't buy it for you. I just want to know *why* you want it. Do you have a reason?"

"I have a reason," she said, very frustrated, "I just don't know what it is." The originality of that answer was good enough for me; I bought her what she wanted.

After Katie started growing a potbelly, Jo found a stockpile of empty candy bar wrappers stuffed into her desk drawer. The curious thing was that she could so easily have gotten rid of those wrappers—if she didn't want us to see them—in any of those KEEP NEW YORK CLEAN baskets that were on every street corner. Why keep *empty* candy wrappers in her desk drawer?

When the three of us sat down to dinner, Jo would say something like, "Honey, don't you think it would be better if you ate this?" or, "better for you if you didn't eat that?"

I asked Margie for advice. She said, "When you talk to Katie, don't talk about food!"

JEAN RENOIR

I received a film script with the oddest title: *Quackser Fortune Has a Cousin in the Bronx.* The script told an unusual story: A cheerful, uneducated young Irishman, in 1959, follows horses all around Dublin, collecting horse manure to sell to middle-aged women gardeners, with whom he occasionally has sexual dalliances. He wakes up one morning to find that all the horses that had been pulling milk wagons around Dublin for years have been replaced by motorized vehicles, and so he loses the only job he ever knew.

When I finished reading *Quackser,* I knew I wanted to do it—but it certainly wasn't the most commercial script I'd ever read. Sidney Glazier, who had produced *The Producers,* was leaving for England that night. I gave the script to him to read on the plane.

He called me from London the next day and said that he wept after reading *Quackser* and that we were going to do it together. Sidney had backing from a wealthy company that wanted to invest in films. (Not Joe Levine's company, thank goodness.)

When Sidney came back from England, I told him that I thought the most important thing for us to do now was to find the right director, preferably an Irishman. The next week, we flew to London, where we stayed at the great Connaught Hotel. It was very difficult to get a room there, but Sidney always managed to get a suite because he brought the manager a special kind of bacon from a gourmet shop in New York. (*That's* a producer.) On this trip he obtained his usual beautiful suite, and I got a little cubicle the size of a cloakroom—but it was a cubicle in the Connaught Hotel. We interviewed many directors, especially Irish ones, but none had a vision that impressed us.

One afternoon, after another disappointing series of interviews, I casually exhaled a loud, "Oh, to find a Jean Renoir somewhere." I pronounced the name correctly, but Sidney was a New Yorker who used to work in burlesque houses.

"Who's Gene Renwer?"

"Oh, just one of the greatest directors of the twentieth century—*Grand Illusion, Rules of the Game*. His daddy was a famous painter."

"Well, let's get him."

"Sure, why don't you just call him up and say, 'Jean, baby, how's about doing a nice little film about a young Irishman who collects horse shit for a living?'"

The next morning Sidney said, "Pack your suitcase—we're going to Paris. We have an appointment tomorrow morning with Gene Renwer. I sent him the script, and he's reading it today." (Now that's *really* a producer.)

We flew to Paris and stayed at the Hotel Raphael that night. The next morning we took a taxi to the address that was given to Sidney over the phone. It was just off Place Pigalle.

I said, "Sidney, this can't be right. That's the Moulin Rouge across the street. We're in a neighborhood of strip joints."

Sidney showed the taxi driver the small piece of paper on which he had written Renoir's address.

"*Oui, oui, oui—c'est là!*" the driver said, pointing to an iron gate.

We got out of the taxi, and Sidney rang a bell that was attached to the side of the gate. I thought some pimp was going to answer. The gate buzzed open and—as in a fairy tale—we walked into a nineteenth-century street lined with tall chestnut trees, behind which were little gardens in front of very old town houses.

Sidney started hollering, "MISSHURE RENWER—HELLO! MISSHURE GENE RENWER!" (I had tried earlier to explain the difference between "Gene" and "Jean" but failed. I didn't attempt to change "Misshure.")

After Sidney had shouted, in his beautiful French, to all the second-floor windows on both sides of the street, a gardener who was working nearby finally pointed to a door. Sidney rang the bell, and the door buzzed open. We walked up one flight of stairs, then another, and then we heard a woman's voice, with a beautiful English accent, call out to us, "Right here, gentlemen—just on the next landing." We were expected.

When we got to the landing, a distinguished-looking woman in her sixties, Renoir's secretary, showed us into the sitting room. She pointed to two chairs that were facing a beautiful desk and asked us to sit down. She was French, but her English was impeccable.

"Monsieur Renoir will be with you in just a moment. May I offer you some coffee or tea?" We both declined.

After a minute or two, Jean Renoir walked in, slowly, followed by his secretary. He must have been close to eighty. His right eye seemed bigger than his left. After his secretary introduced us, she left the room. Renoir had lived and worked in the States, so speaking English was no problem for him.

Renoir sat behind his beautiful desk, with the sun shining through the window next to him, hitting him directly in his right eye. We talked pleasantries for awhile, but when I saw tears starting to drop from the large, red eye, I asked—in as inoffensive a way as I could—if he wouldn't like to change seats with me. "No, no," he said. "The sun feels good on my bad eye."

To break the ice I said, "Monsieur Renoir, do you mind if I ask—which is your favorite restaurant in Paris?"

"Well," he said, "it's an old bistro called Chez Allard. It may not be the best food in Paris, but it's a good restaurant, and the wine is honest."

"So, Misshure," Sidney began, "did you have a chance to read the script?"

"Yes, I've read it. Not since Chaplin have I come across such a character as this Quackser. I'll do your film."

My heart jumped.

"But I cannot do this film for one year," Renoir said, "because of obligations I have. And I know this movie business—you may not have the money one year from now. It's a long time to wait. I know this problem. But, if you still want me . . . I'll do this film."

After we said polite things and how honored we were to have met him, Sidney finished our meeting with, "Okay, we'll keep in touch." We shook hands again, and Sidney and I left the room.

On the way down the staircase, Sidney said, "He's a smart man. He's right, you know—I have the money now, but I don't know if I'll have it in a year from now. It's up to you—you want to take a chance, I'll wait. But it's a chance. You think about it."

I thought about it overnight. I knew this would be the only chance I would ever have to work with Jean Renoir, but I kept thinking of his words: ". . . I know this movie business—you may not have the money one year from now." I thought about Joe Levine and how fickle money people can be. I decided I didn't want to take a chance that *Quackser* wouldn't be made. I told Sidney, "Let's do it now," but for a long while afterward I thought, *What if?*

When we got back to England, we hired an Indian director, Waris Hussein, who lived in London. He had directed some wonderful dramas for the BBC and a lovely film with Sandy Dennis called *Thank You All Very Much.* In May, two months before filming was to begin, I went to Dublin with the author, Gabriel Walsh, in order to study Irish accents. Gabriel was born and raised in Dublin. With my miniature tape recorder I recorded people in all the restaurants and little shops where Gabriel took me. I discovered that there was a great difference in Irish accents, depending on which side of the river Liffey a person lived. The sounds were softer and more poetic in people who lived south of the Liffey, so I decided that when we started filming, I would try to sound like I was born and raised south of the Liffey.

I wanted to live in the countryside when Jo and Katie came to live with me, so I went with the line producer, John Cunningham, to search for a home or a cottage somewhere south of Dublin. Cunningham knew the area very well. As we traveled through a quiet fishing village, called Greystones, we passed a simple, but beautiful home, and I casually remarked, "Now that's the kind of place I'd like to find." Cunningham stopped the car and started to get out.

"Where are you going?"

"To see about that house," he answered.

"But you can't just walk into someone's home and ask them if they'd like to rent it if there isn't even a sign in front."

"Yes you can. In Ireland you can."

He disappeared for three or four minutes and then waved for me to come in.

"It's yours, if you want it. They could use the money, and they have a little place in Dublin they can live in for the summer."

. . . Well, I never.

Two months later we were filming in one of the poorest sections of Dublin, but you wouldn't have known it because the doors and the window frames and the shutters of each house were painted in soft, yet daring, colors—orange, green, blue, red, pink—and everything was extraordinarily clean. I was invited to take a look inside of the house that had been selected as "Quackser's house." We would only be using the exterior, but I wanted to see what it looked like inside. I found that everything was just as clean inside as it was outside. There were three large photographs placed prominently, side by side: John F. Kennedy, the pope, and Robert Kennedy.

Children of the neighborhood gathered around us every day to watch us film. One little boy—a four-year-old named David—was like the mascot of the group. Everyone protected him. He was dressed so nicely, and scrubbed clean, and he always had a stoic face, except if one of us gave him an ice cream; then he would smile, slightly, and say, "Tanks very mooch."

I asked the director if we could use David in one of the scenes. It would mean money for his family. That afternoon he was my sidekick in a very short scene. He just held my hand, and I led him wherever I was supposed to go. The next day I had a slightly bigger scene for him. We were sitting on the step, in front of "my" house, as I was trying to digest the fact that the horses had all been replaced. We had to do the scene several times. David didn't have any dialogue; he just had to sit quietly on my lap. After the fourth take, just as the camera started rolling, he said, "I don't want ta do dis no more."

A month later David's mother started hinting, in the nicest way, that it might be nice if I adopted David and took him to America with me. David was one of eight children. His father was permanently disabled, and the family survived on welfare. His mother wanted David to have a chance in life. I talked it over with Jo and Katie, and they both said it was all right with them. I had the producer make some inquiries. The Irish government said yes, I could adopt David, *but* I would have to wait two years before I could take him out of the country, he would have to keep his own name, and he would have to be raised as a Catholic.

When I got over my anger with the Irish government, I took David for a picnic in the Wicklow Mountains—just the two of us—to find out if he would even want to come with me and live in America. After the most delicate probing, David said, "Naw, I don't want ta do dat." And dat was dat.

I had a scene in a pub where I get drunk on Guinness beer. I like beer once in a while, and I tried getting real Guinness down my throat, but it was so heavy and bitter that I just kept spitting it out. The man in charge of props gave me a stein of Coca Cola and then poured an ounce of Guinness on top. It worked.

When September came around, Jo and Katie had to leave for New York so that Katie could start school again. The weather in Ireland had been beautiful all summer, but by the end of October it became consistently dark and rainy, so depressing, that it could have driven a man to drink. If I had been a drinking man, with hardly any money and little opportunity to improve myself, I might have drowned my cares in beer, but under no circumstances would it have been Guinness.

chapter 18

NEW YORK, NEW YORK

After shedding my manure clothing and exchanging those rags for my New York look—which meant dressing myself in the way that I thought Cary Grant dressed, so that I could fool myself into believing, for a moment when I looked into a mirror, that I looked a little like Cary Grant. I flew back to New York and my reunion with Jo and Katie.

Katie became even more critical of herself and the way she looked. She wasn't fat—she was just "ten years old chubby." So was I at her age, and I was ridiculed by a few snotnose kids in grade school who used to call me Fatso. The scar remains.

Katie would ask if I thought she was going to be a fat pig when

she grew up. I told her—and meant it—that I wasn't worried
about her being too heavy; I was worried about her becoming too
thin when she grew up. She had no idea what I was talking about.
I kept remembering the little love note she handed me on the day
we moved into our first home together: "I love Gene. He is thin. He
is handsome." That was when she was only seven and a half. I was
a good prophet because when Katie grew up, she was thin and
beautiful.

Another pattern started to become a habit. The night before a
big exam at school, Katie would beg for help. I tried to reason
with her.

"Honey, you can't cram all this into your head overnight. This is
    something you needed to study two or three weeks ago, when
    they told you about the exam."
"What good is that going to do me now? The test is tomorrow
    morning."
"But what about the next time this happens?"
"I don't care about the next time—I need your help now."
"But what if the same thing happens next month?"
Then she would start to cry.
"WILL YOU STOP TALKING ABOUT THE NEXT TIME? ARE
    YOU GOING TO HELP ME OR NOT?"

So, Jo and I would take turns helping her—enough for her to
get a passing grade, and to quiet her growing anger.

I'm not a disciplinarian. I understand the need for discipline, of
course, but I'm just not good at it. I'm not talking about hitting—I
don't think any parent should ever hit a child—but about setting
the rules and sticking by them. How to punish without taking
away love—that's the great art. I wished that I could do it, but I
was trapped by the most ironic dichotomy: I was afraid that if I set

rules and drew lines and enforced discipline, Katie would take her love away from me.

MY EPITAPH

Although I liked Roald Dahl's book *Charlie and the Chocolate Factory*, I wasn't sure if I wanted to play Willy Wonka. The script was good, but there was something that was bothering me. Mel Stuart, the man who was going to direct the movie, came to my home to talk about it.

"What's bothering you?"

"When I make my first entrance, I'd like to come out of the door carrying a cane and then walk towards the crowd with a limp. After the crowd sees that Willy Wonka is a cripple, they all whisper to themselves and then become deathly quiet. As I walk towards them, my cane sinks into one of the cobblestones I'm walking on and stands straight up, by itself . . . but I keep on walking, until I realize that I no longer have my cane. I start to fall forward, and just before I hit the ground, I do a beautiful forward somersault and bounce back up, to great applause."

". . . Why do you want to do that?"

"Because from that time on, no one will know if I'm lying or telling the truth."

Mel Stuart looked a little puzzled. I knew he wanted to please me, but he wasn't quite sure about this change.

"You mean—if you can't do what you just said, you won't do the part?"

"That's right," I answered.

Mel mumbled to himself, ". . . comes out of the door, has a cane, cane gets stuck in a cobblestone, falls forward, does a somersault, and bounces back up . . ." He shrugged his shoulders. "Okay!"

When I got to Munich—where the filming had already begun—Mr. Stuart showed me the entranceway to "Wonka's Chocolate Factory." I had practiced my forward somersault on a gym mat for three weeks before coming to Munich. The Scenic Department had made three Styrofoam bricks that looked just like cobblestones, which they laid into my entrance walk. That way I wouldn't have to hit the exact same brick with my pointed cane every time we did the scene. On the day they filmed my entrance, I did the scene four times, in just the way that we had planned. Then Mr. Stuart asked me to do *just one* without the cane. I took a deep breath, swallowed my better instincts, and did the scene without the cane. The next day, David Wolper—the head of the studio—watched the rushes of my entrance. As I was coming out of the commissary after finishing my lunch, Mel Stuart ran up to me.

"He loved it! David loved it!"

"What if he hadn't loved it?" I asked.

"Well, I would have used that take without the cane."

It's not that David Wolper doesn't have good artistic judgment—he does, and he loved what he saw. But if it had been Joe Levine who was bankrolling the film, I think he probably would have said, "What the hell's that guy doing with a cane? Where the fuck does it say that Willy What's-His-Name is a cripple?" I understood better why artistic control is so important to directors.

By the end of November I was glad to get back to New York, but, like most actors, the glow of having just completed a big job wore off quickly and I wondered if I would ever be asked to do another film. I began writing my second screenplay, *Tough Guy*. It was about a B picture movie actor who plays a very cool tough guy, fighting against crooks, but when he comes up against some actual crooks offscreen, it's a little different. That script was never produced.

KOSHER PORK

I was asked to do publicity in Chicago for the release of *Willy Wonka*. Chicago was only ninety miles from Milwaukee, so I went home to see my father and his new wife, Belle. She and her husband had been good friends with my mother and father before her husband died. After my mother died, my father couldn't even raise his arm high enough to comb his hair—bursitis, he said—but when he started dating Belle, you'd think he was doing commercials for a hairbrush company.

The night I arrived in Milwaukee, Belle cooked a delicious brisket of beef. The next morning a huge limousine drove up in front of my father's small house. All the homes in this quiet neighborhood were small, but attractive, middle-class homes. My father couldn't believe the size of the automobile that was parked in front of his house. He got in, and we were driven to Chicago. He had never ridden in a limousine before.

Paramount Pictures was distributing *Willy Wonka,* and they provided a beautiful suite at the Ambassador East Hotel—home of the famous restaurant, the Pump Room. We weren't staying in Chicago overnight—the beautiful suite was just for interviews with the journalists. When work was finished, I took my father to dinner at the Pump Room. My stepmother's daughter and her husband lived in Chicago, so I invited them to join us. It was a beautiful dinner, ending with a flaming dessert—everything paid for by Paramount Pictures. My father couldn't believe all of this splendor.

I held my father's hand on the ride home that night. After about half an hour of cheerful bantering back and forth, he got quiet. Then he said, "I always told you not to put all your eggs in one basket. Since you were a little boy, I warned you not to put all your eggs in one basket. Now I'm glad you did." What I didn't have the heart to tell him was that *Start the Revolution Without Me* and *Quackser Fortune* had both failed at the box office, and if *Willy Wonka* also failed, I didn't know where my next job would come from, or even if there would be a next job.

I took the opportunity of this sweet ride home to ask my father one question that had always bothered me.

"Daddy, you remember when I was sixteen and had just come back from the Reginald Goode Summer Theater and wanted to buy some ham when you stopped at a delicatessen? Why did you put up such a fuss over buying a little piece of ham?"

He took a long pause.

"I was only eleven years old when we came over from Russia. When we settled in Milwaukee my mother used to tell all of us kids that if we ate pork we'd get sick and vomit."

"But you *did* eat pork."

"Whaddya mean?"

"Whenever we went to Mammy's Restaurant . . . you and I would always have the spareribs."

"So?"

"So where do you think spareribs come from?"

"A cow."

"Daddy, it said on the front of the menu, 'Pig on the Cob—our specialty.'"

"Well—that doesn't count."

"Well what about when you made bacon for us on Sunday mornings?"

"Well bacon is different. That's not really pork."

"What do you think it is, Daddy?"

He grew silent for awhile; then he said, "Jerry . . . my mother didn't know from 'spareribs' and 'bacon'—she didn't even know how to speak English—she only knew about pork chops and ham. I never thought about getting sick from eating spareribs or bacon because she never said those words."

I squeezed his hand a little tighter and wished that I had asked my question a little earlier.

The next day I got a call from Woody Allen, at my father's home in Milwaukee.

"I want to do a remake of *Sister Carrie*," he said. "I'm thinking of either you or Laurence Olivier in the man's part, but instead of a woman in Jennifer Jones's part, I want to use a sheep."

He had my number—both my father's phone number and my acting number. I knew before reading the script why he wanted me—an actor who could believably fall in love with a sheep and play it straight.

Before I left for Los Angeles to do Woody's film, I found out that *Willy Wonka* had failed at the box office. It seems strange now to think that Roald Dahl's morality story wasn't embraced. I was told that many mothers thought the lessons in the movie were too cruel for children to understand. As the years since have proven, children don't have any trouble understanding the movie—they crave to know what the boundaries are. It was the mothers who had a little difficulty.

By now I had three commercial flops in a row. Four, actually— *The Producers* suffered because of a bad review from a reviewer named Renata Adler, who wrote for the *New York Times*, so Joe Levine sold the movie to television to get more money to advertise his other movie, *The Graduate*. Renata Adler called Mel Brooks's movie "black college humor." She left the *Times* after a short stint, but it was too late. She did go on to an illustrious career at the *New Yorker*, but I wish she had left the *Times* a year earlier.

Struggling to be a genius is endemic to young artists who are starting their careers, but after being bloodied a few times, they just hope that they won't be ridiculed in the press or on television by those few who have the power to coronate them or tear them down.

I remembered a quote from Gary Cooper: "I need one movie out of three to be a hit." I was leaving for California to do Woody's film in hopes of resurrecting my career.

EVERYTHING YOU ALWAYS WANTED TO KNOW ABOUT SEX

Apart from "Good morning" and "Good night," Woody said only three things to me during all of the filming of *Everything You Always Wanted to Know About Sex*.

1. "Did anyone offer you tea or coffee, Gene?"
2. "Do you know where to go for lunch?"
3. "By the way—if you don't like any of these lines, just change them to what you'd like to say."

It seemed an extraordinary thing to say. As we worked, I realized that Woody's great confidence was not that he knew he'd chosen the right actor, but that the *event* he'd written was more important than the particular words the actor used to bring that

After Woody's film I came back to New York and made appoint-

THE DEMON IS DEAD.

After Woody's film I came back to New York and made appointments to see Margie on what used to be our regular Tuesdays and

Thursdays. The afternoon before our first appointment, she called me at home, which was rare, to say that she needed to change our appointment to a later date. I said, "Well, I'll try to hold out that long." She answered with something like, "Well, it'll give me a break from having to listen to you when you get boring."

I thought about that sentence for the rest of the day. Her remark irritated me so much that I decided I wasn't going to go back to her—and then my good sense told me that if I had learned anything from Margie in the last seven years, it was to deal with a problem at the time it happens, not to hide it away in the corner of my mind, to noodle over for weeks and months.

I walked into her office on the morning she requested.

"I didn't think you'd show up today—after what I said to you on the phone."

"I didn't intend to come back, but I thought that not showing up wasn't a very healthy way to end a relationship. I came to tell you in person that I'm not coming back."

"Sit down, Gene . . . please."

I sat down, facing her.

"I asked myself why on earth I said that to you. After I hung up I felt sure you wouldn't come back. Then I realized that it was my way of letting go of you."

"You were letting go of *me*?"

"That's right. The therapist has to let go, too, you know—not just the patient. It was time . . . but I didn't realize it until I insulted you that way. You don't need me anymore, Gene."

I was very touched. We talked for the rest of the hour. I asked some questions that I had put off for a long time, concerning my marriage and a growing sadness I was experiencing.

"Gene . . . when you told me how much you loved Mary Jo, I said, 'I think she's a terrific woman, but are you sure you want to get married?' "

"I still don't know what that means."

"It means that you were a twenty-three-year-old semivirgin who got into a hopeless marriage with Mary because some friend of yours got his girlfriend pregnant. Yes?"

". . . Yes."

"And a few minutes after you got your divorce from Mary you fall in love with Mary Jo, who may or may not be the right person for you—I don't know—but you immediately start to feel guilty if you don't ask Jo to marry you because her daughter starts calling you 'Daddy.' Yes?"

"Yes."

"What you do about your marriage is your business—now tell me about your Demon."

"My Demon is dead. I drove a stake through his heart—he'll never come back. I don't question my own goodness anymore."

"Do you know why the Demon came in the first place?"

"I think so."

"Tell me."

"What right did I have to be happy—sexually or any other way—if my mother was suffering every day of her life? I think the Demon timed his arrival very cleverly, just when my hormones were screaming to be free. I prayed my guts out instead of letting my sex out. And my anger."

Margie was silent for a few moments. Then she gave me a soft smile.

"You know, Gene . . . just because you're leaving doesn't mean you can't call me or write, or come to see me if you ever need help with something."

I looked at my watch.

"Time's up, Margie."

I got up, and we hugged each other. I whispered, "Thank you."

"BEFORE IT'S TOO LATE"

Westhampton Beach, Long Island, is deserted in the winter and spring. I thought it would be nice to go there in the off-season, on weekends and during school vacations, so I rented a small cottage.

The day before Valentine's Day Katie and I had just gotten back from grocery shopping and were about to get out of the car, but she looked so sad and just sat still. I asked her what she'd like for Valentine's Day, knowing that the answer would be some kind of chocolate.

"I want a five-pound box of chocolates."

I started to laugh, until I saw that she was deadly serious.

"Five pounds! Honey, five pounds would be enough for—"

"If it isn't five pounds, don't bother. I don't want any!"

"You mean, if I got you a one pound box of beautiful chocolates you'd throw it away?"

"Yes. Or two pounds, or three pounds, or four pounds." Her eyes started tearing.

"I WANT FIVE POUNDS—or else don't get me anything!"

Katie got out of her car and headed for the front door. I caught up with her and hugged her. I tried to kiss her, but she pulled her face away.

"I can't give you five pounds of chocolate, Katie—I wouldn't be a good father if I did that."

"You're not my real father anyway."

She knew exactly where to place the dagger. I just stared at her. She burst into tears and cried out, "Hit me! For God's sake, hit me—before it's too late."

The next day I bought two heart-shaped boxes of chocolate, one for Jo and one for Katie—*one pound each.* Katie ate her chocolates as if we had never had that horrific conversation, but the phrase "before it's too late" stayed with me. It was a cry for help; I understood that. But I was afraid it was also a cry of anger that could take her away from me.

chapter 19

THE BIRTH OF A MONSTER

During Katie's Easter vacation we went to Westhampton Beach for several days. The memory of *Everything You Always Wanted to Know About Sex* was so happy that it was making me sad—wondering if I would ever be asked to work in something wonderful again.

After lunch one afternoon I walked up to my bedroom with a yellow legal pad and a blue felt pen. At the top of the page, I wrote, *Young Frankenstein,* and then wrote two pages of what might happen to me if I were the great grandson of Beaufort von Frankenstein and was called to Transylvania because I had just inherited the Frankenstein estate.

Why the word "Young" before the name "Frankenstein"? It came out almost unconsciously, but when I asked myself, later, where that thought came from, I remembered Mickey Rooney in the film *Young Edison,* which I saw when I was a boy. Then I remembered a more recent clue: Anne Bancroft had made a film called *Young Winston.*

That evening I called Mel Brooks in New York and told him my little Frankenstein scenario. "Cute," he said. "That's cute." But that was all he said.

When summer came, I rented a small house on the bay in West-hampton Beach. On our first Saturday night, Jo and Katie and I watched a summer replacement television show called *The Marty Feldman Comedy Machine.* After seeing it I felt like saying, "Who was that masked rider?" but instead I said, "Who is that funny man with the strange eyes?"

A week later, I received a call from my California agent, Mike Medavoy (this was before he became a famous mogul). He said, "How about a film with you and Peter Boyle and Marty Feldman?"

"How did you come up with that idea?" I asked.

"Because I now represent you and Peter and Marty. Have you got anything?"

"Well, that's a wonderful, artistic reason to make a movie, but, as it happens, I think I do have something."

"What?"

"No, I want to work on it for another day. I'll send it to you."

That night—inspired by having just seen Marty Feldman on television—I wrote a scene that takes place at Transylvania Station, where Igor and Frederick meet for the first time, almost verbatim the way it was later filmed. I sent off my four typewritten pages to Medavoy. He called two days later.

"I think I can sell this. How about Mel Brooks directing?"

I told Mike that I didn't think Mel would direct anything that he hadn't conceived. The next day, I got a call from Mel.

"What are you getting me into?"

"Nothing you don't want to get into."

"I don't know, I don't know—I'm telling you, I don't know."

The next day, Mike called.

"Mel said yes. I made the deal. You're supposed to write and then send Mel every twenty pages. Congratulations!"

Mel had spent two years working on *The Producers,* for which he received the total sum of fifty thousand dollars. Then he spent two years working on *The Twelve Chairs,* for which he also received a total sum of fifty thousand dollars. Both films failed at the box office. If either one of those films had been a commercial success, I don't believe Mel would have said yes to *Young Frankenstein.* Lucky me! Lucky Mel!

Medavoy was the one who got me into writing. On my day off, when I was filming with Woody, Medavoy and I literally bumped into each other on a street corner in Beverly Hills—in front of a clothing store called Carrol and Co.—and he asked me if I'd like to have tea with him someday.

"Is that your way of saying 'I'd like to steal you away from whoever's representing you in California and have you sign with me'?"

". . . Yeah," he said. "You should be writing your own stuff."

Because of that accidental bump on the street corner, Mike Medavoy became my California agent. A few months later, after Woody's film, Mike called me in Westhampton Beach and said, "How about a film with you, Peter Boyle, and Marty Feldman?" That's Hollywood.

Everything You Always Wanted to Know About Sex came out in 1973 and was a big success. Again I thought of Gary Cooper's quote: "I need one movie out of three."

Mel was in California doing preproduction on a film he had

lined up before *Young Frankenstein;* it was called *Black Bart.* The title was later changed to *Blazing Saddles.* He sent me a copy of the script.

When Mel had a week off, he came to New York and wanted to have one working session on *Young Frank,* as he always called it. He came to my place, and we spent forty-five minutes making coffee and discussing the merits of different brands while we ate little *rugelachs.* This was a ritual with Mel before anything serious could be discussed. (He preferred Kentucky Blue Mountain coffee, and I preferred Columbian White Star.)

While we were having our coffee and *rugelachs,* Mel asked me to play the part of Hedley Lamar in *Black Bart.* I said, "Oh Mel, I'm all wrong for that part—but how about Jim, the Waco Kid?"

"No, no, that's Anne's favorite part, too. No, I need an older guy—someone who could look like an over-the-hill alcoholic. I'm trying to get Dan Dailey."

"Mel, there are so many wonderful comics who would be much funnier than I could ever be playing Hedley Lamar."

And that was the end of my being in *Blazing Saddles.* (Or so I thought.)

When coffee matters were finished, we went into my study and talked for about an hour about *Frankenstein.* The next day Mel took off for Los Angeles to start filming *Blazing Saddles,* and I started writing *Young Frankenstein.*

DOCTOR FRANKENSTEIN MEETS LILY VON SHTUP.

At the top of the first page of *Young Frankenstein,* I wrote, "In black & white." I didn't know if I had a chance in hell of seeing that dream realized—since most studios insisted that films be made in color—but I thought that if Mel fought for it hard enough, we might have a chance.

While I was writing, I realized that we needed a really frightening woman to open the huge door of the Frankenstein castle. I tried to think of someone from real life, or film, to use as a model. The woman who scared me the most from all the movies I had seen in my youth was Mrs. Danvers in Hitchcock's *Rebecca*. Mrs. Danvers was played by Judith Anderson—the woman who also scared me when I was fifteen and went to see her in *Medea*.

Now I needed a good name for my Mrs. Danvers, so I took out a book of letters written to and from Sigmund Freud and found that someone named BLUCHER had written to Freud. After *Young Frankenstein* opened and was such a big success, people asked me if I knew that the word *blucher* in German means "glue." But the truth is, I never dreamed that the name had any meaning—I just liked the sound of it . . . a name that might frighten the horses when they heard it. (The horses knew what I didn't.)

After I finished about half of the script, I left for Los Angeles to do the film *Rhinoceros*, with Zero Mostel. I showed Mel the fifty-eight pages. He just said, "Okay. Now let's talk about what happens next." I assumed he liked the pages, but I wasn't sure. For about an hour we discussed what might happen next. Then we said good-bye.

When I got back to New York, I started writing the second half of *Young Frankenstein*. Shortly after I finished the first draft, I got a call from Stanley Donen, who asked me to please come to his office and meet Alan Jay Lerner. When I got there, Stanley asked me to do the part of the Fox in the movie of Saint-Exupéry's classic book, *The Little Prince*. He said, "You can play any part you want, but I think the Fox is the best part." I read the script, adapted by

Alan Jay Lerner. The Fox was certainly the best part for me, and I said I would be happy to do it.

I had met Stanley Donen a year earlier, when we were both boarding a plane to New York. My agent, Mike Medavoy, had sent him the first script I'd ever written, called *Hesitation Waltz,* to see if he was interested in directing it. He wasn't, but when we were getting onto the plane, he introduced himself and suggested that we sit together for the ride to New York.

"You should direct that script yourself."

"But I don't know how to direct."

"I'll bet you do," he said as we were getting into our seats and fastening our seat belts. "Let's watch whichever movie they're showing today—but don't put on your headphones."

When the film came on (it was a Don Knotts comedy), Stanley started asking me questions.

"What do you think of the lighting in this shot?"

"No good."

"Why?"

"Well . . . it looks flat. There doesn't seem to be any mood to it, or any focus."

During the next scene he said, "Tell me about the shadows."

"Well, there's something wrong—but I can't tell you what."

"Do you see that one shadow is coming from the left and the other is coming from the right?"

"Yes."

"It could never happen that way in life—only in the movies. The cameraman didn't decide where his light source was coming from."

And so on, for the rest of the movie. During that plane ride, Stanley gave me my first lesson in directing. From that time on, if I was supposed to approve or reject a director for some film I was going to do, and I didn't know the director's work, I would watch a video of a previous film the director had made, and I would watch it *without sound* so that I wouldn't be led astray by how beautiful the music was or by how good or bad the dialogue was.

When I got back to New York, I started writing the second half of just as I was about to leave for a little vacation with Jo, before going to London to do *The Little Prince,* Mel called from a soundstage at Warner Bros.

"I need you right now!"

"What's the matter?"

"Dan Dailey begged off doing the Waco Kid because he was too tired, so I got Gig Young. But Gig started foaming at the mouth on the way to his first scene in the jail cell. I thought he was just doing some preparation for the part—I said, 'Keep doing what you're doing'—I didn't know he had just gone on the wagon. We had to send for an ambulance to carry him out. I yelled, 'IT'S A SIGN FROM GOD!' I'm calling you from a pay phone next to the set— can you come right away?"

"Mel, I have to be in London in two weeks to do *The Little Prince* for Stanley Donen."

"Call him up! Ask if you can come later!"

I called Stanley in London and told him the situation. He said, "Do you really want to do Mel's film?" I said, "I really want to help Mel if I can." Stanley said, "All right—I'll shoot your scenes at the end of the schedule instead of at the beginning." I left for Los Angeles the next day.

The following day I was looking at Cleavon Little, who appeared to be upside down, since I was hanging upside down in a jail cell.

"Are we black?" I asked.

The greatest thrill I had in *Blazing Saddles* was watching Madeline Kahn, as Lily von Shtup, singing "I'm Tired." During the film-ing, I suggested to Mel that Madeline would be wonderful in *Young Frankenstein.*

Of course, if Stanley Donen couldn't rearrange his filming schedule, I wouldn't have been in *Blazing Saddles,* and I wouldn't have met Madeline Kahn, who, a little later, played my fiancée in *Young Frankenstein* and my love interest in *Sherlock Holmes' Smarter Brother.*

chapter 20

LE PETIT PRINCE

Before I left for London to do *The Little Prince*, I went to Milwaukee to visit my father, who was seriously ill. I tried to make him laugh, telling him about Mel Brooks and *Blazing Saddles* and Dom DeLuise singing, "Stick out your tush"—but when I kissed him good-bye, I knew I was seeing him for the last time. A week later I was told that my father had died. I was filming in an enormous artificial wheat field on a huge soundstage, delivering the most memorable lines in the script:

"It's only with the heart that one can see clearly; what's essential is invisible to the eye."

A week later, I sang and danced in the English countryside with a six-year-old boy. Stanley Donen had choreographed a beautiful tango for this little prince and me.

* * *

When I got back to New York, the anger in Katie was showing it-self in more hurtful ways, which she usually took out on her mother. I was caught in the middle so often that I felt like a referee in a boxing match—a match where only one boxer was trying to hurt the other, because Jo never wanted to hurt Katie, no matter how much she was being hurt herself.

Young Frankenstein was sold to Columbia Pictures. I was thrilled. I flew to Los Angeles to work with Mel. When I saw him, he said, "Think you're pretty good, huh?"

I tried to hold back a smile as I said, "Yeah."

"Well, I got news for you, Jew boy—now the work begins."

We would meet each evening, and—after the coffee ritual—we would discuss what I should work on the following day. "YOU DON'T HAVE A VILLAIN! You understand what I'm saying? WE'VE GOT TO HAVE A VILLAIN! Otherwise there's no story tension."

The next morning I would start writing. By late afternoon—if I thought I'd written anything worthwhile—I'd type up the pages. Mel would come over after dinner each evening and look at the pages.

"Okay. NOW! We've got to change the structure. YOU CAN'T GO TO TRANSYLVANIA JUST BECAUSE YOU GOT A LETTER TELLING YOU ABOUT THE WILL. . . . SOMEBODY'S GOT TO COME TO YOU *FROM TRANSYLVANIA—WHILE YOU'RE GIV-ING A LECTURE—*AND HE HANDS YOU THE WILL."

In all the time we spent together, we had only one argument. I can't even remember what it was about; I just remember that he yelled at me. Ten minutes after he left, he called me on the phone from his house: "WHO WAS THAT MADMAN YOU HAD IN

YOUR HOUSE? I COULD HEAR THE YELLING ALL THE WAY OVER HERE. YOU SHOULD NEVER LET CRAZY PEOPLE INTO YOUR HOUSE—DON'T YOU KNOW THAT? THEY COULD BE DANGEROUS."

That was Mel's way of apologizing. We've never had another argument since that time. Disagreements occasionally, but not arguments. The only other time I thought we were having an argument was when I showed him a scene I had just written in which Dr. Frankenstein and the Monster sing and dance to "Puttin' On the Ritz." After he read it, he said, "ARE YOU CRAZY? You can't just suddenly burst into Irving Berlin. It's frivolous!"

I argued logic, from Dr. Frankenstein's point of view: his need to win over this stuffy audience of scientists and their wives with incontrovertible proof that the Monster could be taught to do anything. This was apart from the logic of giving the movie audience a burst of dazzling entertainment. I argued until my face started to turn from red to blue. After about twenty-five minutes of this, Mel suddenly said, "Okay—it's in!"

I was flabbergasted. "Mel, how can you argue with me for twenty-five minutes and then just casually say, 'Okay—it's in!'?"

"Because I wasn't sure—do you understand? I wanted to see how hard you'd fight for it. If you gave up right away, I'd know it was wrong. But when you turned blue—I knew it must be right."

WALK THIS WAY.

Columbia Pictures insisted that the budget for *Young Frankenstein* not exceed $1,750,000. The budget we had arrived at came to $2,200,000. Mel and I, along with our producer, Michael Gruskoff, thought of things we could cut—things that we didn't want to cut, but that might get the budget down. ("Puttin' On the Ritz" might have been one of the sacrificial lambs.)

On the morning of our meeting with Columbia Pictures, the three of us were waiting in a small reception room, talking about what else we could possibly cut from the script, when Mel suddenly slapped his head and cried out, "WE'RE NUTS! We should just go in there and say, 'You guys are crackerjacks. Your budget is *right on the nose*. So I'll tell you what—you come up $200,000, we'll come down $200,000, and we'll meet in the middle. Two million!' "

We walked into the office of John Veitch, who was the executive in charge of this meeting. He was also a smart man and a gentleman. After listening to Mel he said, "That's fair. Let's do it."

But the man at the head of Columbia Pictures said NO! He gave us two days to find another studio that might do our picture with our budget, but if we couldn't find one, we had to cut our budget down to their demand—*and not one penny more*. Michael Gruskoff gave the script to his friend Alan Ladd, Jr., at 20th Century-Fox, where we made the film for $3,000,000.

We never improvised dialogue on the set. Physical actions, yes, but not dialogue. One day we were filming the scene of Madeline Kahn's arrival at the Frankenstein castle. She was wearing a fox stole and a big turban on her head. The scene seemed flat to all of us. After we tried several things, Mel suddenly said, "Marty! When Gene says, 'Eyegore, help me with these bags,' you say, 'Soitanly—you take da blonde, I'll take da one in da toiben.' "

We all laughed and started the scene again, on film. I said my line, Marty said his, and then Marty—in one of his impulsive inspirations—took a huge bite out of the tail of the fox fur that Madeline was wearing around her neck, but the tail came off in his mouth. We all had to go on playing the rest of the scene while we looked at Marty with a tail in his mouth. Out of such lunacy great comedy is born.

When we were filming the Transylvania Station scene, in which "Eyegore" leads me off of the platform to the hay wagon, Mel suddenly said, "Marty, bend over as you walk away with your little cane and tell Gene, 'Walk this way.'"

"What does that mean?" I asked.

"I'll tell you later."

We did the scene. Everyone laughed, but I still didn't know what it meant. After we finished the scene, Mel said, "Man walks into a drugstore and says to the pharmacist, 'I got terrible hemorrhoids—have you got some talcum powder?' Pharmacist says, 'Yes sir—walk this way.' Man says, 'If I could walk that way, I wouldn't need the talcum powder.'"

I hate to think what might have happened if we had been forced to make the film at Columbia. As it turned out, Alan Ladd, Jr., asked Mel and me to sign five-year contracts at Fox.

Making *Young Frankenstein* was the happiest I'd ever been on a film. Madeline Kahn, Peter Boyle, Marty Feldman, Teri Garr, Cloris Leachman, Kenny Mars . . . and Mel directing. It was like taking a small breath of Heaven each day.

I'm always lonely when I'm on my own—a leftover I think from the Demon, who always struck when I was alone—but towards the end of filming I realized that I was going to be lonelier when I returned to my home and family. On the last day of filming, during our lunch hour, I was sitting in the Frankenstein bedroom set, staring at the fake fireplace. Mel wandered in and saw me.

"What's the matter? Why so sad?" he asked.

"I don't want to leave Transylvania."

"AND IF THAT HORSE AND CART FALL DOWN . . ."

When I got back to New York, I made an appointment with Margie.

ME: I want to leave Jo.

Margie didn't say anything; she just waited.

ME: Katie always came first with Jo. . . . Well, she was her daughter before I came along, so I can understand it. Jo marries a drunk and a liar who she kicks out after she finds out she's pregnant with his child, and then she spends her whole life trying to make it up to Katie. I can understand that. I think it might ruin both of their lives—but I can understand it. I was always a very loved "number two" . . . but after what I went through with my first marriage, I want to be number one. It's not noble, I know that—but I want to leave.

MARGIE: So leave.

ME: I won't if it's going to do damage to Katie. I don't mean hurt— I mean damage.

MARGIE: You want to know if she'll survive? She'll survive! Living with someone who doesn't want to be there would do more harm.

Telling Jo that I wanted to leave was the cruelest thing I've ever done in my life. I knew in my heart that I had to leave, but how do you explain such a thing in a way that won't cause pain? What difference did it make how I explained it—I was sticking a knife into her, and she never saw it coming. "You tell Katie why you're leaving us, and I want to be there when you tell her."

The three of us sat in my little study. I stumbled my way through some kind of an explanation that I knew couldn't change the fact that I was leaving. When I finished my tortured monologue, Katie ran upstairs to the nearest phone, filled with excitement. I could hear her telling her girlfriend the news, almost as if she were joining a club and was going on a great adventure. Her girlfriend's parents were also divorced.

Sometime later I found out that Katie had gone to see Margie and told her that she knew I was going to leave. She thought it was because of Madeline Kahn. Where she got that notion from, I have no idea. Perhaps when Katie visited the set of *Young Frankenstein,* she saw us rehearsing one of our comic love scenes. . . . I still don't know the answer. I loved Madeline, but I never looked twice at her romantically—except in the movies, where I adored her.

On June 6, 1974, I left my home and family.

MONSTER RIOT

Mel hired John Howard as editor for *Young Frankenstein.* John had edited *Butch Cassidy and the Sundance Kid* and *Blazing Saddles.* After seeing a film put together for the first time, a director usually wants to vomit (you may be thinking "ixnay on the omitvay," but I assure you it's true) because it doesn't have any of the rhythms the director had in mind while filming.

When I arrived in Los Angeles, I got a hotel room and an office at 20th Century-Fox and then joined Mel each day in the editing room to look at whatever John Howard had put together. When we saw the ascension scene—where I rise with the Creature on an elevated platform and cry, "LIFE, DO YOU HEAR ME? GIVE MY CREATION LIFE!," my heart sank. I thought this was going to be one of the highlights of the film, and instead it was a boring blob. I put my head down. Mel didn't vomit. Instead, he got up and started banging his head against the wall. He hit it three times, hard. Then turned his face to the rest of us and said, "Let's not get excited! You have just witnessed a 14-minute disaster. In one week you're going to see a 12-minute fairly rotten scene. In two weeks you're going to see a 10-minute fairly good scene. And in three weeks, you are going to see an 8-minute masterpiece."

That's a cute speech, I thought, *but you're kidding yourself, or just trying to make us feel better. How much can you change without reshooting? I saw the scene. I don't believe in miracles.*

The next three weeks were my second lesson in directing: thousands of little pieces of film can be arranged in thousands of different ways. Almost three weeks to the day after Mel's speech, the lights went out in the screening room, and I witnessed an 8-minute miracle.

While we were still filming *Young Frankenstein,* I told Madeline and Marty that I had an idea for a romantic comedy, with music, about a brother of Sherlock Holmes. I wanted to write parts for both of them, but I didn't want to start writing unless they both wanted to do it. When they said yes, I started writing *The Adventure of Sherlock Holmes' Smarter Brother.*

During the editing of *Young Frankenstein,* I worked on *Sherlock* in my office in the mornings, sat with Mel in the screening room in the afternoons, and in the evenings went to a little French restaurant, called La Chaumiere, where I continued writing *Sherlock* with a long yellow legal pad, a blue felt pen, and a glass of Sancerre.

The first time I had seen Teri Garr was when she came to read for the part of Inga, my laboratory assistant in *Young Frankenstein.* Mel called her "the long-legged beauty." Teri's father had been Eddy Garr—a semifamous comedian who had worked as a second banana to Phil Silvers for several years. In her audition, Teri's Transylvania accent was so funny, and her acting was sensational. Although I had never seen her father, I used to think that Teri must have inherited his great comic timing. When all the auditions for Inga were over, Mel asked me who I wanted in the part. No contest: "The long-legged beauty."

When I settled in Los Angeles and started my new life, I asked Teri to go out with me. She was not only beautiful on-screen, she was beautiful offscreen—always full of life and humor, and always very sensitive. Eventually we became lovers. One evening she played an album of songs for me by someone I had never heard of . . . Randy Newman. I was so taken with him that I wanted to buy the album the next day. I couldn't understand how it could be that I had never heard the songs of this wonderful black singer.

"He's not black," Teri said.

"Oh, I'm sure he is. . . . Just listen to him."

"No, he's not black."

I felt like a fool when I finally met him. My only defense is that he doesn't talk the way he sings, and I wouldn't want to change anything about the way he sings.

I went to see Teri perform on the *Sonny and Cher* show—where she appeared regularly—and found out that Teri was also a dancer. It was a sweet comfort to be with such a pure and gentle woman, who could laugh and love and remain unspoiled by the smog of show business that hung over Los Angeles.

Young Frankenstein opened in New York at the Sutton Movie Theater in December of 1974. I flew to New York for the opening and took Katie with me. It was a midnight screening on a Thursday so that the movie could qualify for the weekend grosses, and I was very nervous. The lights dimmed, and when the title YOUNG FRANKENSTEIN appeared onscreen, the audience started clapping before a word was spoken. I relaxed. The movie was a big hit and Mel and I received Academy Award nominations for writing.

chapter 21

SHERLOCK HOLMES HAS A JEWISH BROTHER.

When we were in the thick of editing *Young Frankenstein,* Mel had asked the editor to put in a close-up of Teri Garr as she watched me strangle Eyegore for stealing the wrong brain.

John said, "We don't have a close-up of Teri in this scene, Mel."

"What are you talking about?"

"You never shot one."

I thought Mel was going to start banging his head against the wall again, but he just turned to me and said, "Don't you ever make a mistake like this when you're directing."

"But I'm not directing."

"YES, you'll see, you'll see. . . . If you keep writing, you're going to want to direct, just so someone doesn't screw up what you've written. If it makes a few bucks, they'll let you do it again; if it bombs out, they won't."

John Howard solved the problem of "no close up" of Teri for the strangling scene by taking a close up of her from another scene—in which she was wearing the same white lab coat—and he put it in where Mel wanted. You would never know if you didn't know.

Two weeks later Alan Ladd, Jr. (known as Laddie by almost everyone) asked me if I wanted to direct *Sherlock Holmes' Smarter Brother.*

Paul Mazursky's office at Fox was around the corner from mine. I admired him as a director, and when I told him that I was going to London to direct my first film and I wanted his help, he gave me one piece of advice: "Get to know your production designer!"

I went to London with my producer, Richard Roth, to start pre-production. I stayed at the famous Connaught Hotel again—just like old times, except that this time my room was a little larger. The representative of 20th Century-Fox in London said, "Gene, you can meet any production designer in England that you wish; all I ask is that you see Terry Marsh first. You two are twins."

The next day, Terry Marsh walked into my hotel room. We talked about his work on *Lawrence of Arabia* (which had brought him an Academy Award nomination), *Doctor Zhivago,* and *Oliver* (he won Academy Awards for both), and after about twenty minutes I felt as if I had found my long-lost brother. I loved the English accent, of course, but the simple way he described complicated things and the humor with which he described them, won me over.

It's egotistical to write, direct, and act in your own film, but it's also necessary. If you aren't any good and the picture bombs, you won't be doing that egomaniacal job again. But, as Mel said while

editing *Young Frank,* "If it makes a few bucks, they'll let you do it
again." I was now doing what Leo Bloom said he wanted: "Everything I've ever seen in the movies."

I had a comedy scene at the beginning of filming "Sherlock"
that was one of my favorites. I thought it would be a cinch. This
was the setup: I'm waiting to see Lord Redcliff in his study. There
is a tempting box of chocolates, sitting open on his desk and melt-
ing in the sun. I take one piece of chocolate, and it's delicious, so I
decide to steal just one more tiny piece. But I accidentally knock
the whole box onto the floor. I kneel down to pick up the candies
and, just as I've grabbed most of them in my hand, I hear footsteps
approaching. I cram all of the gooey chocolates into my mouth
and stand up to shake hands with Lord Redcliff. My face and
hands are covered with chocolate, and when I try to talk, my
speech is muffled, because my mouth is stuffed full of chocolate.

Now, you'd think that this scene would be fairly easy for me—
just give me some good chocolate, which the prop department
did. But every time I tried to speak after stuffing the chocolates
into my mouth, nothing intelligible came out. I tried putting less
and less chocolate in my mouth, but that made it impossible not to
swallow most of it as soon as I started talking, and the comic
essence of the whole scene was that I was trying to talk normally. I
finally came up with the strangest solution: I asked for a bottle of
Perrier, took a small swig, and held the water in my mouth without
swallowing. Then I nodded to the assistant director to call, "Action." My speech sounded a little bizarre, but you could understand everything I was saying, and I was able to hold the water in
my mouth without swallowing it. The crew was holding back
laughter, but all I was trying to do as an actor was to speak as normally as I possibly could. It was the same lesson I had learned
from Chaplin, when I saw *The Circus:* If the physical thing you're

doing is funny, you don't have to act funny while doing it. . . . Just
be real, and it will be funnier.

During three months of rehearsals and prerecording our songs,
Dom DeLuise kept us laughing. When the actual filming started,
he kept the whole crew laughing, not just with his acting but also
between takes. He is the funniest man, in person, that I've ever
known.

I had never met Albert Finney, but he did me the great favor of
acting a tiny part in one scene. He sat as a member of the film audience that was watching a slapstick Italian opera. Albert had one
line to say: "Is this wonderfully brave, or just rotten?" After his
scene was over, we made plans to see each other again. During that
summer I became good friends with Albert and his wife, Anouk
Aimée. They were very loving with each other, but Albert is a big
talker and Anouk had to fight with him for equal time.

Katie came to visit me for a week during filming. She was sixteen now and had matured a great deal. It was probably the happiest week we had ever spent together. She came to work with me
each morning—early as it was. She got to know the crew, watched
the filming, laughed at Dom DeLuise . . . and loved the attention
that the handsome young men on the crew were paying her. In the
evenings Katie and I went to little restaurants near Berkley Square,
which were a few streets away from where I lived. No arguments,
no temperamental bursts . . . just fun. By the end of the week, I
thought we had crossed the Rubicon.

When the filming of *Sherlock* was over, my editor—Jim Clark—
told me to go away for a few weeks while he put the rough cut together. "Then it'll be all ready for you to vomit when you see it for
the first time."

My New York agent, Lily Veidt, had sent me a postcard from a beautiful chateau in the Provençal hills. The postcard had a photo of the chateau, and she circled a little balcony on the photo and wrote, "If you ever need a good rest, come here." Albert Finney had told me about a wonderful hotel restaurant in the same area, called La Columbe d'Or, where Simone Signoret and Yves Montand usually stayed during the summer months. So I went to Chateau St. Martin for two weeks.

On my second night in France, I drove to the village of St. Paul de Vence and walked into La Columbe d'Or. It was an outdoor restaurant, jam-packed with people, mostly tourists, who were sitting under the fig trees that surrounded the terrace. I had made a reservation and was looking for a waiter or maître d' to tell me where to sit, when suddenly I was enveloped by a mass of purple. I couldn't see anything but purple and didn't know what was happening . . . until I heard the words, "Monsieur Bloom! Monsieur Bloom!" When the purple receded, there was Simone Signoret, embarrassed for what she thought was the spectacle she had made of herself. She apologized and explained that she had shown *The Producers* to her nieces and nephews so many times and suddenly—in walks Monsieur Bloom.

She led me over to her table—where she sat each evening—and introduced me to her guest, James Baldwin, with whom she was having dinner. She said that Mr. Baldwin was guiding her while she wrote her first book. She asked me to join them for a drink after I had eaten.

I sat, eating my baby chicken with *chipolata,* thinking of how funny my "purple meeting" must have looked to all the people watching, and how thrilled I was to have been enveloped by one of the greatest actors of our time.

After I had my drink with them and said good night to James Baldwin and was kissed by Simone Signoret on both cheeks, I went outside, walked close to my car, and threw up on the street. It wasn't about the food. I may act brave and sometimes outrageous—on screen—but in real life I get terribly nervous when I meet the great talents whom I've admired for years from afar.

I was in Paris on a Friday when I received a phone call from Laddie telling me about a script he wanted me to do. It was called *Super Chief*. But he needed to know my response immediately, because another actor wanted to do it and had given Fox until Tuesday to decide. Laddie had someone fly to Paris that night in order to hand me the script the next morning. When I was halfway through reading it, I called Laddie and said yes. The title was later changed to *Silver Streak* because the Santa Fe Railroad—which owned the actual Super Chief—thought the movie would give train travel a bad name. (*Au contraire, mon cher.*)

Sherlock Holmes' Smarter Brother opened at Christmas week in 1975 and was a big hit.

chapter 22

CRISIS IN BLACK AND WHITE

There was one scene in *Silver Streak* that I thought might be its Achilles heel—when I'm in the men's room putting on shoe polish, trying to pass as black. Before casting started, I told Laddie that I thought there was only one person who could play that scene with me and keep it from being offensive, and that was Richard Pryor. Laddie said, "That's who we want."

I met Richard in Calgary, Canada, the night before our first scene together. We were both checking in at the Holiday Inn reception desk when we saw each other. No high jinks, no trying to be funny—just a very warm handshake and an expression of admiration for each other's work.

IMPROVISATION

The next morning we did our first short scene. There were police cars and helicopters and guns all around us. I jumped into a ditch next to him—as I was directed to do—and Richard said his first line, and I answered. Then he said some line that wasn't in the script, and I answered with a line that wasn't in the script. No thinking—just spontaneous reaction. That was the start of our improvisatory relationship on film.

I had never improvised onstage in front of a paying audience—only in class—but in 1968 I worked with Elaine May and Renee Taylor to raise funds for Eugene McCarthy in his quest for the presidency. Renee and I would meet in Elaine's apartment and, after Elaine set the situation—that we were all at a cocktail party talking about the upcoming election—Elaine turned on her tape recorder and we improvised for ten or fifteen minutes. The next night we met again. Elaine had typed up the best bits from the previous night's work, showed them to us, turned on her tape recorder, and we improvised again, using those best bits from the night before as signposts. After working this way only three times, we were ready to tour the country, improvising each night at whichever college or home we performed in.

So many beginning actors who want to improvise usually aren't improvising at all—they're just trying to think up clever lines, and then the competition sets in with the other actors to see who's going to come up with the funnier line.

During *Silver Streak* words kept coming out of my mouth in response to things that Richard was saying—things that weren't in the script. Of course, Richard was used to working this way from all the jobs he had done in clubs and concerts. I don't say that Richard's way is without any thought—but his method always has an emotional, rather than intellectual, base. In this regard, Richard was my teacher: no thinking—just immediate, instinctive response. If it's no good, the director will cut it out—assuming you have a director who wants you to improvise.

Strasberg used to say that improvisation was just a tool, like a hammer or a screwdriver or a file, to be used only if you're having trouble in a scene, or if the director thinks that something is wrong in the script. Then you might be asked to improvise, which is to say, "speak other thoughts"—thoughts between the lines—that you, the actor, are feeling in the situation. But of course, "If something isn't broken, don't fix it." Improvising for the sake of improvising usually leads to banalities or irrelevant jokes.

At six o'clock in the evening, on the day before our big "shoe polish scene" in the train station, Richard and I went into the men's room with our director, Arthur Hiller, to rehearse the next morning's work. We started going through the lines of the scene—very lightly—and Richard suddenly went somber. He didn't say what was wrong. Arthur Hiller didn't notice it, but I knew Richard fairly well by then, and I knew there was something churning inside of him. After the rehearsal, Richard and I walked across the street to the Royal York Hotel, where we were both staying.

"What is it?"

"Nothing. Too late."

"Just tell me what it is."

"It's too late, Gene."

"Tell me."

"I'm going to hurt a lot of black people."

"How?"

"Doesn't matter. It's too late."

"It's not too late. We can talk to Arthur; I can call Laddie . . . but you have to tell me what it is."

"You're a nice guy, Gene, but I don't want to talk about it. And I don't want to do this film. I want to get out of it."

"I'm in room 1504, Richard. If you change your mind, just call me."

"Good night, Gene."

Fifteen minutes later the phone rang.

"This is Richard. You mind if I come down and talk with you?"

Richard came into my room.

"White man comes into the toilet to pee, sees you wearing shoe polish, thinks you're black, naturally, 'cause that's how all niggers look."

"Richard, did you read this scene before we started rehearsing today?"

"I guess I must've, but it didn't mean anything to me then. Sometimes I get somebody to read scenes to me."

"What would you like the scene to be?"

"Should be a *black* man who comes in to pee, sees you, knows right away you're white, sees you trying to keep time to the radio music, and says, 'I don't know what your problem is, mister—but you gotta keep time.'"

"That's a better scene," I said.

I picked up the phone and called Arthur Hiller. That night he hired a black actor. The next morning we shot the scene just the way Richard described it, and the movie didn't shut down.

The Concise Oxford Dictionary

sullen: passively resentful, gloomy-tempered, not responding to friendliness or encouragement, melancholy.

If the dictionary had added, "brilliantly funny, often exhibiting warmth and affection" . . . it could have been defining Richard Pryor.

MY OLD BEAN

During *Silver Streak,* we would occasionally film in parts of Canada that were high up in the snow, and there would be long waits between shots. While I was waiting in my trailer, with the heater on full blast, I started writing a script from a new idea I had about a baker from Milwaukee, in 1927, who wants to try out for a big Hollywood contest to find the next Rudolph Valentino. He takes his wife to Hollywood, tries out for the part, and his wife runs off with the real Rudolph Valentino. Years earlier I had seen a film by Federico Fellini, starring Alberto Sordi, called *The White Sheik,* which had inspired this idea. I called my script *The World's Greatest Lover.*

When *Silver Streak* was finished filming, I was in Paris for a week, doing publicity for the opening of *Young Frankenstein* in France. (The French called it *Frankenstein Jr.*) Since I had *The World's Greatest Lover* on my mind, I decided to call the legal department at 20th Century-Fox to find out if we had to worry about being sued—because my idea was inspired by *The White Sheik.* They told me I would have to have some kind of permission from Fellini—just to play it safe. My dear friend Denise Breton—who worked in Paris doing publicity for Fox—said, "I know Federico—let's call him up." She picked up the phone in her office, and two minutes later I heard the voice of the great Fellini.

"I loved your *Frankenstein.* It was a great movie. You are a great actor."

"Thank you. Signor Fellini, I need—"

"Federico! Please!"

"Thank you. Federico, I have a little problem. I was inspired by *The White Sheik* and wrote a film called *The World's Greatest Lover,* and even though my story is almost completely different from yours, the legal department at 20th Century-Fox says I need some kind of permission from you—just in case."

"Okay, Gene—here's what you do: on the screen, in the opening titles, you write—in big letters—AND SPECIAL THANKS TO MY FRIEND FEDERICO FELLINI. That will take care of everything."

I did as he instructed. When the film opened and the audiences saw those lines . . . they laughed, thinking it was my little joke. But it wasn't a joke. That's what Federico wanted—that's what he got. And I didn't have any legal problems.

I asked the Art Directors' Union to allow Terry Marsh to come to the United States to design *The World's Greatest Lover*. With his credentials it wasn't difficult to get permission.

Terry came to Los Angeles with his wife, Sandra, and when filming was almost finished, they saw a little house in Sherman Oaks and wanted my opinion as to whether they should buy it. It was a simple, but beautiful, small house, in perfect condition. I said, "Take it!" They bought the house and stayed in Los Angeles. Terry designed all of my films, plus *Basic Instinct, Hunt for Red October, Shawshank Redemption. Clear and Present Danger,* and several films for Mel Brooks.

In the Hitchcock film *Suspicion*—which Terry and I once saw together—Cary Grant and Nigel Bruce always call each other "old bean" or "old chap." Whenever I make a long-distance call to Terry, I always start out by saying, "Hi, old bean," and he always answers, "How are you, old chap?"

Terry and Sandra Marsh are both American citizens now, and have a beautiful home in California . . . all because one man in London said, "Gene, you can meet any production designer in England that you wish; all I ask is that you see Terry Marsh first. You two are twins."

MEETING YOUR IDOL

Silver Streak was a big hit and was chosen as the Royal Performance for the queen of England and the royal family. I couldn't go to London because I was filming The World's Greatest Lover at the time, but a month later, when Prince Charles came to visit 20th Century-Fox, I was invited to attend a luncheon in his honor, to be held in the Fox commissary.

As I was walking along the small street that leads from the office buildings to the commissary, a taxi pulled up and I heard someone shouting, "Oh, Mr. Wilder! . . . Mr. Wilder!" I turned and saw Cary Grant stepping out of the taxi. My heart started pounding a little faster, but I didn't throw up this time, as I did when I met Simone Signoret. Cary Grant walked up to me, and after we shook hands, he said, "I was sailing on the QE II to England with my daughter, and on the second day out she said, 'Dad-dy, I want to see the Silver Streak—they're showing it in the Entertainment Room.' And I said, 'No, darling, I don't go to movies in public.' And she said, 'Dad-dy Dad-dy, please—I want to see the Silver Streak.' So I took her to see your film. And then we saw it again the next day, and the next. Tell me something, will you?"

"Of course."

"Was your film in any way inspired by North by Northwest?"

"Absolutely! Collin Higgins, who wrote the film, loved North by Northwest. It was one of his favorites. I think he was trying to do his version of it."

"I thought so," Mr. Grant said. "It never fails! You take an ordinary chap, like you or me . . . (An ordinary chap like you or me? Didn't he ever see a Cary Grant movie?) . . . put him in trouble way over his head, and then watch him try to squirm out of it. Never fails!"

———

In 1976 I saw John Hurt portray a man named Quentin Crisp in the television dramatization of Mr. Crisp's book *The Naked Civil Servant.* I thought it was astonishing. I had never heard of Quentin Crisp. When I read that he was performing his own one-man show in Los Angeles, I bought tickets and went to see *An Evening with Quentin Crisp.*

The first act was mildly interesting, but not very exciting. Mr. Crisp had obviously worked out every move and gesture. There was no spontaneity to it. Just before the intermission he invited the audience to fill out cards and ask him any questions they wished. When the short intermission was over, he came back onstage and started reading the cards. Then he came to this one: "Mr. Crisp, what right do I have to enjoy my life when there are so many people all over the world who are starving and in pain?"

The Demon flashed through my brain: the memories of praying for hours at a time, the Vaseline in my hair, the feeling that people thought I was a freak as they watched me pray in front of buildings—and all I was really asking God was this same question.

Quentin Crisp shaded his eyes and looked out into the audience.

"Where are you, dear?" he asked. "Please stand up."

A young girl—perhaps twenty years old—stood up.

"How old are you, if you don't mind my asking?"

"Nineteen," she said.

"Oh, my dear . . . my dear girl . . . you'll find that if you take care of the person on your left and the person on your right—you'll have a full-time job."

I wished that some wise person had given me this same advice when I was nineteen and going through the torments of my Demon. But, of course, it wouldn't have made the slightest difference . . . not until I could come to that simple epiphany on my own. I hear you, Margie: "Bravo, *Mister* Wilder."

chapter 23

LEO BLOOM HAS HIS PICTURE TAKEN.

When I was making *Sherlock Holmes' Smarter Brother* in London, Peter Sellers called and asked if we couldn't take a little walk in the park some Sunday afternoon. I said it would be a pleasure.

We went to Green Park and—as I walked along a little stream amongst all the ducks and pigeons—I saw that Peter was taking pictures of me. He explained that, apart from his acting, he was also a professional photographer and that he just wanted a few mementos. After awhile I noticed that every time I heard the camera click, I was in some Leo Bloom pose. Peter told me that he and George Harrison exchanged a copy of *The Producers* every two weeks.

Peter and I had dinner together several times during that year. Once, when I was in Stockholm doing publicity for a film, he had a woman friend of his call me at my hotel—I suppose she was a Swedish beauty—who asked if I wouldn't like to have some company. (In case you're wondering, I said no.)

I went from Stockholm to Copenhagen for a day and a night, to do publicity for the opening of *Sherlock Holmes' Smarter Brother* in Scandinavia. The biggest lesson I learned during that short time was never to pronounce the city of Copenhagen as CopenHAAgen—the way the Nazis pronounced it—but rather CopenHAYgen. It may seem like a small point, but it wasn't small to the Danes. It also made me wonder why no one bothered to inform Danny Kaye about the correct pronunciation in his film about Hans Christian Andersen, when he sang, "Beautiful, beautiful CopenHAAgen . . ."

While I was in CopenHAYgen, I was interviewed by a lovely woman named Gunilla who worked for a Scandinavian magazine. She was about thirty-five and extremely smart, with a playful smile. She was one of the most naturally cheerful people I'd ever met. I remember thinking that if she were ever to come to Los Angeles on some assignment, I would certainly like to ask her out, but I didn't tell that to Gunilla because I didn't want her to think I was just another one of those typical American men who flirt with all the pretty European women and are actually full of bullshit.

In 1978 I went to Scandinavia again, to do publicity for the opening of *The World's Greatest Lover,* but this time the press junket was in Stockholm, in an outdoor café that 20th Century-Fox had rented. And there she was, sitting amongst all the other journalists, smiling at me. I gave Gunilla a nod and then answered questions for about an hour.

"What are you going to be doing next?" one of the gentlemen from Norway asked.

"A film about a Polish rabbi who comes to America at the time of the Gold Rush and becomes best friends with a bank robber and is captured by Indians."

When the interviews were over and the other journalists were leaving, I went up to Gunilla and shook her hand—holding on to it longer than necessary—as I said hello and good-bye to her. What a shame that she lived in Sweden.

"By the way, Mr. Wilder, I'm coming to Los Angeles to do a series on Hollywood for my magazine."

". . . When?"

"In November, for about a week."

"If I give you my telephone number, will you call me and tell me where you're staying?"

"Yah, sure. . . . I was hoping you might say that," she said with a smile. "Maybe I can do an interview about your new movie."

* * *

The film about the rabbi and the cowboy was called *The Frisco Kid*. The wonderful Robert Aldrich was going to direct, but we still had to find a costar—someone Warner Bros. would approve.

Bob Shapiro—who was vice president in charge of production at Warner Bros. and the man who offered me the film—suggested several names, and I suggested several actors, and Robert Aldrich suggested some more names. In each case, the actors mentioned were either not available or not approved by Warner Bros. Then Bob Aldrich suggested John Wayne.

"Are you kidding?" I said. "How could we ever get John Wayne?"

John Wayne wouldn't read the script until he was offered his usual fee: one million dollars and 10 percent of the gross. After a lot of stupid haggling on the part of Warner Bros., John Wayne was offered what he asked for. To my great surprise, after reading the script he said yes. He also said that he loved that little rabbi.

Apart from being able to work with John Wayne. I was also relieved, because in spite of the presence of the rabbi, with John
Wayne starring, *The Frisco Kid* would be perceived as a Western,
not as a Jewish film.

A few days after Mr. Wayne had accepted, some very experienced Warner Bros. executive went to talk to him, at his home in
Long Beach. A few hours later, John Wayne pulled out of the film.

"What the hell did you do?" Bob Shapiro asked the executive.

"I tried to get him for seven-fifty instead of a million—I thought
we could save a little money."

So we lost John Wayne, and the search for a costar began again.
I was asked to look at the work of an up-and-coming young actor
by the name of Harrison Ford. I thought he was charming and
might possibly get somewhere in the business. Since we all liked
him, he was hired.

DOCTOR STRANGELOVE BREAKS MY HEART.

Terry Marsh was hired as production designer on *The Frisco Kid,*
and Mace Neufeld was the producer. We went to Greeley, Colorado
to film for a week. Since there wasn't much to do in Greeley,
Harrison and Terry and Mace and I went to the Chuck Wagon for
dinner every night. The food was good, but the best part of the
evening came after dinner. The restaurant had a dart room attached, and we all played darts and had an after-dinner drink.

During the filming of *Frisco Kid,* I developed a fondness for Bob
Aldrich. He was smart, and he knew exactly what he was doing all
the time. And like all of the best directors, he left the doors open
for you to surprise him. He liked what I was doing with the rabbi,
and if he said, "Try another one," I knew that what he really meant
was, "Surprise me."

Later, when were filming in southern Arizona, we all went over the nearby border into Nogales, Mexico, for dinner. Bob Aldrich was a gracious host. He would only drink Coca Cola on the set, but when we went out to dinner on a Saturday night, he was a good drinker and a good storyteller. When we got back to Los Angeles, I received a phone call from Peter Sellers.

"Genie, how are you?"

"Fine, thank you, Peter. And you?"

"Fine. Fine. Genie, I want to know what you think of the director, Robert Aldrich. I've been asked to do a farce about lady wrestlers, and I want your opinion of him."

I always get a little nervous when people ask my opinion of an actor or a director—knowing full well that I might have an influence on whether or not someone gets a job. But Peter was one of the greatest talents I had ever seen, and I wanted to honor him with an answer.

"Peter, I get along great with Bob. He's a wonderful director, but you have to understand that my picture is a Western—with shooting and socking and blood and lots of action. How he would be if he were directing a farce, I can't say. He was always wonderful with all the comedy things I did. I loved him."

The next day Bob's daughter, Alida, called me. "How could you have done that to my father?"

"Done what?"

"Blackballed him on the movie he was going to do with Peter Sellers. Sellers told the movie company that Gene Wilder said Aldrich wasn't any good."

Here's my advice: BEWARE OF GREEKS BEARING GIFTS . . . or other actors or directors who ask your advice about someone you've just worked with.

A LITTLE ROMANCE

In December, Harrison and I were filming interiors for *The Frisco Kid* at a studio in Los Angeles. I got home from work one evening, and there was a message from Gunilla on my answering machine, saying that she was staying at a small hotel near the Farmers' Market. She left her telephone number. I called and made a date to see her the next night. It would be a Friday, and I would have the whole weekend off.

After work on Friday I took Gunilla to a very nice, very quiet restaurant. The food was delicious, and, to my surprise, Gunilla was a great eater, even with her slim figure. Over dinner she told me about her two daughters, thirteen and eleven, to whom she was devoted. She had been divorced for several years and basically was raising her daughters on her own. They had occasional visits with their father. I told Gunilla about Katie and a little about my marriage to Mary Jo, but when I thought I was sounding too sad, I changed the subject. I told Gunilla that if she would come to my house for dinner the following night, I would cook the best roast chicken she ever had, plus baked potatoes. She flashed one of her playful smiles and said yes.

I picked Gunilla up at her hotel early Saturday evening. She loved the chicken. I told her how simple it was to make, but she had to use *Spice Islands Garlic Salt* and no other. While we ate, we talked about films, and she told me how badly the Swedish government was treating Ingmar Bergman. There was no mad rush to make love, but when I started talking with a Swedish accent and making up Swedish words, the lovemaking came about slowly and easily. I asked her beforehand if she used any birth control devices, and she said that she had the newest copper IUD, which was very popular in Sweden. The lovemaking was sweet and affectionate.

The *Frisco Kid* company was moving to Santa Barbara on Monday, for two days and a night. I asked Gunilla if she'd like to come along, and she said yes.

We all arrived at a beautiful stretch of beach, and the camera crew set up for the first shot. Santa Barbara was beautiful, but very cold that December day. Harrison and I were dressed in our costumes—long johns—and we waded gingerly into the ocean, which was freezing. While our lips were turning blue, we waited until we heard, "ACTION," and then we ran out of the water, as playfully as we could, and wrestled on the sand. As soon as we heard, "CUT!" the prop department rushed over and covered us with blankets and gave us each a shot of brandy to stop our teeth from chattering. Then we did it all again, two more times.

I stayed with Gunilla in the Biltmore Hotel that night, where it was nice and warm. We ate in the room and made love for the second time. The next day we returned to Los Angeles. Gunilla got on a plane to Sweden, and I left for northern California with the film company.

Two weeks later, while we were filming near the Black River, which was about two hours north of San Francisco, I was talking to Harrison while we sat on our horses, waiting for the next shot. I mentioned that when I was thirteen I had gone to a place in Los Angeles called Black/Foxe Military Institute.

"They've torn the whole place down now, you know."

"Good! I hated that place."

"I bought a lot of the floorboards from the dormitory."

"Why?"

"Well, I'm also a carpenter, and those boards were made from really good wood."

I didn't go into detail with Harrison, but it was eerie for me to think that he might be building a garage, or a child's playroom, using the floorboards from my old bedroom, where I was beaten up and "sort of" corn-holed by Jonesy.

When filming ended, I got a call from my French friend Denise Breton—the woman who had called Federico Fellini for me. She wanted to know if I would like to join her and her family in Paris, in February, and then go to a ski resort near Grenoble during her kids' winter vacation. I was very close with her family, having stayed at their home several times when I was doing publicity in Paris, and even though I didn't know how to ski, I said yes.

A few weeks later I got a call from Gunilla, saying that she was working in Paris for two weeks while her daughters were staying with their father during their winter vacation. I told her that fate must be working its magic, because I was going to be in Paris on February 14, Valentine's Day, just for a night, before I left to go skiing with my French family. We arranged to meet at a little hotel where I used to stay.

RANDOM HARVEST

On February 14 Gunilla and I had a joyful reunion. I had slept on the plane, and since it was a beautiful winter day, we took a long walk along the Avenue Montaigne and looked at all the expensive shops—not inside, just the windows. Gunilla was enjoying our walk, but she seemed preoccupied. I took her to a small restaurant called Chez Edgar, which was around the corner from my hotel. I waited until we sat down for dinner and then said, "Something's bothering you. Please talk to me."

"I'm fine, dear."

"I know you're fine. You Swedes are always fine, except in Bergman films. I'm very smart, you know—about some things. Why don't you tell me what's on your mind?"

"I want you to enjoy your dinner. We'll talk later."

We both ordered escargots to begin and the roast chicken with *pommes frites*. I had ordered some red Bordeaux when we first sat down, but I noticed that Gunilla wasn't drinking any.

"No wine?"

"No, I have a little tummy ache. I'll just drink some water. It's nothing." Then she picked up her glass and tasted the wine, for my sake. "Ooh, yes, it's very nice."

She pecked at her food during dinner, like a bird. It was obvious that the "great eater" didn't feel like eating.

"Some dessert?"

"No, thank you—no, I couldn't eat another morsel."

Now I knew there must be something wrong. Gunilla had brought a little carry-on bag with her, and when we got to my room, she put some things away in the bathroom. She came out wearing a flannel nightgown.

"Now . . . let's have it!" I said. "I've been very patient."

"I'm pregnant, dear."

I had been afraid that she was going to say that she had a serious illness or that something had happened to one of her daughters. Stupid of me. All the signs were right in front of me. A little panic came into my throat, like a bubble.

"Please don't think I'm being coarse . . . but am I the father?"

"Yes, dear. I wouldn't even have told you if I weren't sure of that. There was no one else."

She looked so fragile at that moment, unlike any other time I had seen her. How could she not be frightened? I was frightened too. I put my arms around her and hugged her for the longest time.

"Don't worry, don't worry—you're not alone. We'll figure it out, don't worry."

"I don't know how it happened. My gynecologist said that it only happens with this new IUD maybe once every 100,000 times."

"Well, that's a consolation."

She laughed. I pulled down the cover and fluffed up the pillows. Then we both got into bed, and I held her.

"I don't want to make trouble for you," she said. "I'm so sorry."

"Please don't say that. You have nothing to be sorry for."

"You're not angry, dear?"

"Of course not. Please don't talk like that again. We'll figure out what's best. Don't worry now."

And I held her until we both fell asleep.

The next morning she gave me her telephone number at the magazine where she worked. I already had her home phone number. She told me what an awful boss she had at work and that "if a man answered—hang up." I didn't know she knew that line. We gave her boss the nickname of Pickle Puss. She was leaving that afternoon for Stockholm, which was only a short flight from Paris, and I was meeting my French family at the train station, where we were taking the wagon-lit to Grenoble. Their car was already on the train. From Grenoble we would drive up the mountain to Alpe d'Huez—on the tortuous curved road made famous by the Tour de France. I told Gunilla that I would call her at her home that night—providing I hadn't fallen off a mountain.

I called Gunilla at 6:00 P.M.

"Let's talk honestly," I said. "I know the big question for you must be whether or not to keep the baby. Yes?"

"Yes, of course."

"And I think you must wonder if I want to get married, before you can make such a decision. Is this what you're thinking?"

"Yes, dear, I am thinking those things, but I'm also thinking whether or not I want to have another child . . . to raise another child. My girls are growing so fast. It would seem strange to start all this baby business over again." (She laughed.) "I just don't know. But I want to know how you feel."

"Well, I was married once, when I was quite young—I didn't tell you about that. It was a horrible marriage. And then I was married again to a wonderful woman—I told you about her and her little girl, who is a big girl now. I don't know if I'll ever get married again, but I know that if I do . . . if I do . . . I want to make sure that it's for the right reason. Whatever you decide about the baby, I'll help you, emotionally, financially . . . you know what I mean . . . but I know that I mustn't get married again if I don't think I could be a good father. Does that sound very selfish?"

"No, not at all. I think what you're saying is wise."

"When do you have to decide?"

"The doctor says he'd like to know by the end of the week."

"Have you told your girls yet?"

"No, not yet. I don't want to tell them until I'm sure what I'm going to do."

"Okay. We'll keep talking . . . each evening at six. And if I don't call, you can talk things over with Pickle Puss."

She laughed and then said, "Good night, dear."

The next day I started skiing lessons, using the Graduated Length Method—which meant starting out with tiny skis that were about as long as ice skates. The next day the skis were going to be about two and a half feet long; the next day, three feet. By the end of the week, I was supposed to graduate to about five feet and be able to glide down the mountain like a champion. When I called Gunilla that night, I told her about my little skis and that I'd probably be a champion by the end of the week. And she told me that she had made the decision to have an abortion.

I called her each night at six. On the day of the abortion, she sounded weak, but in good enough spirits to make me laugh when she told me how she had fooled Pickle Puss by telling him that the reason she couldn't come to work was because she had to meet a big movie star who was going to give her an exclusive interview about his love life. By the end of the week she was back at work and sounding wonderful, and I was gliding down the mountain like a gazelle, falling on my face only three times.

chapter 24

SIDNEY POITIER AND I GO STIR-CRAZY

A famous producer by the name of Hannah Weinstein read an article in a newspaper about a rodeo that was held in a prison. She took the writer, Bruce J. Friedman, for a visit to the prison. When they got back to New York, Bruce wrote the first draft of *Prison Rodeo*. Months later, the title was changed to *Stir Crazy*.

I got a call to meet with Sidney Poitier, who was going to direct the film. To say that Sidney and I got along would be like saying, "Food is good sometimes." I loved him. I loved his brain, I loved his humor, and I loved his cashmere sweaters. I don't think I've ever seen him when he wasn't wearing a cashmere sweater—except when he was wearing a tuxedo.

Sidney and Hannah Weinstein and Columbia Pictures wanted

Richard Pryor and me to star in *Stir Crazy,* and after we both agreed to do it, Sidney wanted the script rewritten to accommodate the particular talents of his two stars. He had a black writer friend whom he asked to write a second draft. When he was happy with the structure of the script, he asked me to write my own dialogue, while he wrote Richard's lines—just as a blueprint—knowing that everything was going to change when Richard and I started doing what he called our "stuff."

On the first day of filming, Sidney asked Richard and me to sit down on one of the steps of the prison set. He said that this scene—where we both walk into prison for the first time and then flip out—was probably the most difficult acting scene in the movie and that he thought it would be best to do it on the first day of filming, because of all the adrenaline that actors pump out on the first day of any film. Then he said, "I want you both to fly. I've got three cameras set up, so you can move anywhere, within reason, without worrying about hitting your marks. Do whatever you want; say whatever comes out, but fly. That's why you two guys are here . . . to fly."

And we flew.

Now here's a question I've never been able to answer: why did we both start humming the Laurel and Hardy theme music at the exact same moment at the end of the scene, after we had made a shambles of the prison and the prison guards? Who knows? I suppose silliness has its own method of communication, and Richard and I were certainly silly together—at least on film. The timing of everything we did on-screen came so spontaneously to us that it was *almost* like sexual attraction, in the sense that you don't analyze why you're attracted to someone—it's just chemistry.

But as close as we were on film, it didn't carry over to our private lives. Richard traveled in his own circle. You could count on one hand the times that we saw each other when we weren't working, and even then there was always a work-related reason why we met.

We went to Arizona to film the interiors of *Stir Crazy* in an actual prison. From Tucson, where we all stayed, it was an hour-and-a-half drive to the Arizona State Penitentiary. Sidney used real prisoners as extras. They had all been cleared by the prison authorities to work with us, and each prisoner was paid for every day he worked.

Richard stayed in a private house during our stay in Tucson. Sidney and I stayed at the Arizona Inn. After the first day of filming at the penitentiary, Richard started coming in late. At first it was fifteen minutes, then half an hour, then an hour, then more. I was upset at the insult to the cast and crew and to me, and I thought that Sidney was going to burst because of the time we were losing. But we both knew that if either one of us yelled, Richard would probably just walk out. When Richard would finally arrive on the set, he was all smiles, happy-go-lucky: "How ya doin'?" So Sidney and I put on our happy faces, and the work began.

After a few days, Richard demanded a helicopter to take him to and from work. I didn't blame him for wanting to avoid traveling the hour and a half each way, but it was unfair to the rest of us, who did have to make that long trip. When we finished our two weeks of filming in Arizona, we went back to the pleasures of working in a Hollywood studio.

One day during our lunch hour in the last week of filming, the Craft Service man handed out slices of watermelon to each of us. Richard and the whole camera crew and I sat together in a big sound studio, talking and joking. Some members of the crew used a piece of watermelon as a Frisbee, and tossed it back and forth to each other. One piece of watermelon landed at Richard's feet. He got up and went home. Filming stopped. The next day, Richard called and asked for Sidney and the whole camera crew, and me, to assemble in the studio. When we were all sitting there—like children in a kindergarten class—Richard walked in, introduced us to his aunt or grandmother—I'm not sure which—and then announced that he knew very well what the significance of watermelon was and why that piece of watermelon was specifically thrown at him. He said that he was quitting show business and would not return to this film. He got up and walked out, leaving us stunned. There was no filming the next day.

The day after that, Richard walked in, all smiles, happy-go-lucky: "How ya doin'?" I wasn't privy to all the negotiations that went on between Columbia and Sidney and Richard's lawyers, but the camera operator who had thrown the errant piece of watermelon had been fired. We finished the remainder of the film that week. Richard and I hugged good-bye. It's difficult to continue loving someone who shits on you—but I did, because of the moments of magic that we had shared together.

I assume now that Richard was using drugs during Stir Crazy. The whole country found out a short while later that he freebased cocaine and set himself on fire. That doesn't endear him to me, but at least it helps explain why some of his behavior was not malicious—just crazy.

If Columbia Pictures had not succumbed to Richard's demands, and if I were a cocky, son-of-a-bitch movie star, and if Sidney Poitier had not held in his rage, there would have been no Stir Crazy. For the sake of my psychological health, I should have let out my anger at the time that I was angry. From the point of view of getting the picture made—I'm glad I didn't. The picture was a great success.

chapter 25

HANKY-PANKY WITH ROSEANNE
ROSEANNADANNA

Sidney Poitier and I wanted to work together again. When *Stir Crazy* was finished, we would often meet in the afternoons at the home of my dear friend, Julann Griffin, to play tennis and talk about movies. Julann and I had worked together in summer stock in the north woods of Wisconsin years before, when I was seventeen.

I would play two sets with Sidney (we were very evenly matched) and then talk about what we'd like to do next. I had one script that had been sent to me that I liked very much. It was a comedy/mystery called *Traces*. (The title was later changed to *Hanky Panky*.) I gave the script to Sidney, and he said, "Let's do it." After the success of *Stir Crazy*, I think Columbia would have done almost anything that Sidney and I wanted to do.

Now came the search for the Girl. Lots of female stars said they would do the movie if they could play my part. I know the feeling. One day Sidney called and asked if I would like to go to New York with him to see Gilda Radner in a play called *Lunch Hour* that she was doing on Broadway, directed by Mike Nichols and also starring Sam Waterston. I said, "I don't have to go to New York—I've seen her on *Saturday Night Live* and think she's wonderful." So Sidney flew to New York, saw the play, and took her to dinner. He called me that night.

"She said yes."

"You mean that was it? . . . She didn't want anything rewritten, or to meet me?"

"No. I just told her that she would love you."

When Sidney got back to Los Angeles, I told him that I thought the woman's part had to be rewritten specifically for Gilda, because as it existed it was white bread—more of a straight part. "That's why the other actresses wanted to play *my* part." He agreed.

The day Gilda and I met—or rather the evening we met, because we were going to film at night—was August 13, 1981. The sun had started sinking below the Hudson River when Gilda was dropped off at our location, where the ocean liners docked on the East River. I had already done two close-ups so I was in my makeup and dressed in a tuxedo when I walked up to her to say hello. She was sitting on one of those tall director's chairs, talking with Sidney. Remembering our first meeting was something like a he said/she said situation: *Gilda said* that I rubbed my crotch against her knee when I asked her if I could bring her some tea or coffee. When she told me this crazy story, *I said*, "You're nuts!" And *she said*, "No, they were *your* nuts." Well . . . it was a beginning.

CHILDHOOD FEARS

The moment of sexual decision came after two weeks of filming in New York. I was staying at the Carlyle Hotel, in a room on the nineteenth floor that I always requested. One evening—just so I could get to know Gilda a little better before we started filming our major scenes—I invited her to have dinner with Corinne and my brother-in-law, Gil, at their favorite Italian restaurant on East Sixty-fourth Street.

Gilda looked exceptionally pretty in the light summer dress she wore that evening, which barely covered her skinny knees, and while we all ate dinner, "Gilda Live" entertained us with her slightly raunchy humor, à la Roseanne Roseannadanna. We all laughed, but the people sitting at the table next to us laughed the loudest. The husband of one of the couples was getting tipsy and started sending after-dinner drinks to our table, followed by a stream of suggestive notes—not to Gilda, which we assumed at first—but to my sister, which made our table laugh so loud that the whole restaurant turned to see what was happening.

After dinner Gilda and I said good night to Corinne and Gil and then walked the few blocks to the Carlyle Hotel, where I knew Gilda could get a taxi. It was a beautiful summer evening, and we walked slowly. Horace, the doorman at the Carlyle, told me that a messenger had come from Columbia Pictures with an envelope for me and that it was in my room. I knew it was the script changes for the next day's filming. Gilda said she'd like to see them, just to know if there was anything for her in them. So Gilda came up to my room and looked at the blue pages with me. There were only the silliest little changes—about where the trailers would be parked and where lunch would be served—hardly worth sending a messenger to deliver. Just as I was about to escort

Gilda back to the lobby, she threw me onto the kingsize bed and
jumped on top of me.

"I have a plan for fun!" she said.

I bounced back up.

"And I have a plan for an adorable little girl who's going home."
She threw me back down and jumped on top of me again.

"Come on, come on—you'll like it!"

I bounced back up again, took hold of her shoulders, and
looked into her magnificent brown eyes.

"Maybe I would—it's actually very possible—but I don't wish
to be an adulterer. *Vous comprenez?*"

She mumbled about what a spoilsport I was as I escorted her to
the lobby, gave her a kiss on the cheek, and helped her into a taxi.

Early the next morning I went to the abandoned warehouse that
Columbia Pictures had rented where Hair and Makeup and all
the actors' trailers were parked. I knocked on Gilda's trailer door
to say good morning and see how she was. When I walked in,
Gilda introduced me to her assistant, Mary, and then asked her to
leave the trailer until she called. Then Gilda started talking non-
stop.

"I've only been married a little over a year, and he's a dear,
sweet man, and I care about him—I really do care about him—
but he's very troubled right now, and I'm starting to go crazy.
When he drove me to the movie location the night that you and I
met, I cried the whole way in, all the way from Connecticut, because I knew I was going to fall in love with you and leave my
husband."

"Wait! Now wait a minute Gilda, please!"

"It's true—I swear to God." And she took a big sip out of a flask
she always carried with her.

"Gilda, you're talking like this is a fairy tale, and you're going to meet Prince Charming, and everything's going to be all right, and we'll both live happily ever after."

"So what's wrong with that?"

Her honesty was startling. I tried not to laugh.

"What's wrong is that you don't know me. And I certainly don't know you—although I feel like I'm taking a crash course right now. Everybody loves you as soon as you say hello—don't you know that? Don't you ever meet any nice men who make you happy?"

"I meet so many dumb jerks you wouldn't believe it, and they ask me to come to England with them or come on their yacht or come to Brazil, and then all they really wanna do is drink champagne, snort coke, introduce me to their girlfriends, and tell their other friends that the famous Gilda Radner is here—'You wanna meet her?'"

She took another swig from her flask.

"What's in that?"

"Taste it."

I took the smallest sip. It wasn't bad, and it wasn't very strong.

"What's in it?"

"Tab and vodka. I just take it to calm down a little."

"But it's eight-thirty in the morning."

"It's okay, I'm not addicted. I never get tipsy or drunk or anything. I know my lines, I'll be good. It's just to calm me down a little."

"Gilda, if your marriage is so bad why don't you get out of it?"

"I'm afraid to be alone."

LET'S INVITE ALBERT.

When we were on location in Tucson, Arizona, again, Sidney and his family and Gilda and I stayed at the Arizona Inn. My room was next to Sidney's; Gilda's room was across the courtyard, on the second floor. I still had my feelings about not wanting to be an adulterer, but Gilda's sad marital circumstances and the desperation I saw in her every time we met made me stop focusing on me and adultery. With a proper invitation I would occasionally visit her room at night.

After the last shot of the day—from whichever outdoor location we were filming—I would call ahead to the Arizona Inn and make a reservation in the dining room for Gilda and me. By the time we arrived, most of the other guests had gone, so Gilda and I had the dining room almost to ourselves.

A strange pattern developed, which at first I just thought was cute. Gilda was always tempted by two things for appetizer and two things for her main course and could never seem to make up her mind which ones to order. When the pattern repeated itself each day, I suggested that we simply tell the waitress that our friend Albert was going to be joining us and could we please also order for him, since the kitchen would be closing soon. So Gilda and Albert and I had dinner together for two weeks—even though Albert never showed up. On days when we finished filming early, we'd get to the dining room, and our usual waitress would just say, "And what will Albert be having tonight?"

During one of our dinners together, Gilda told me about another problem that was torturing her, but she didn't want to tell me what that problem was *yet*. I immediately thought it must be about food, but it seemed unlikely that something as trivial as food could be "torturing" her. I tried to persuade her to tell me, but she always said, "I will, I will—just not yet." Then I started to think it was drugs.

It was wonderful to be with Gilda—most of the time—but her excessive need for attention and admiration was overwhelming. I would ask her, "Why on earth are you spending all of your energy trying to make people like you when anyone you meet loves you immediately?" She would just say, "Really? Honest?" Or, "I know, I know—I just don't want to disappoint them."

In one of the sad moods that came over her frequently, she would say. "Is that all there is?" She had heard Peggy Lee sing the song with that title, and it made a great impression on her.

"What more do you want, Gilda? You have so much."

"I know, I know," she said, and she looked at me like a child who had received only one small present for Christmas, and then she said, "But is that all there is?"

After awhile she became desperate to be with me *all of the time*. I was never bored during the next two months—exhausted several times, but never bored. As much as I loved being with her, I wanted to breathe again without having to worry about her. She was so strong willed, and yet so fragile. I started to look forward to the end of filming. When it finally came—at Burbank Airport—we kissed good-bye. She cried. Because she didn't want to take a chance that her husband would answer the phone *if* I should ever want to call her about something personal, she handed me the telephone number of her manager, Bernie Brillstein, and said that if I ever *did* want to see her again, I should call Bernie and say something like, "The ducks are quacking in the pond." I think she really did live in a fairy tale. I kissed her good-bye again. She cried again, and then flew to New York.

After our last good-bye I drove to my home in Los Angeles, feeling that a great weight had been lifted off of me. Gilda was certainly the most extraordinary woman I had ever met—not the prettiest, not the sexiest, not the most considerate, but the most generous and compassionate and original person I had ever known. She was a firefly who glowed in the dark *and* in the light.

I got to my place just after midnight and sat outside for a few minutes, just to breathe a little night air. It was such a relief not to have that needy, clinging baby pulling at my shirt sleeve every minute

I woke up the next morning and went about my business, shopping for milk, toothpaste, socks, orange juice, English muffins, marmalade. Nothing exceptional happened during that day. I made a few calls and met one of my friends for dinner. When I got home, I turned off most of the lights in the house and started walking through the living room toward the bedroom. I stopped next to my piano for a moment, happy to see it again. I started taking off my sport jacket—and suddenly froze. I stood like a zombie, with my sport jacket half-off, staring into space. I didn't know what was happening to me. After a few moments I dropped to my knees and started beating the floor with my fists. Tears flooded my heart. I hate even the thought of drugs, but Gilda had become like some kind of a drug to me, as surely as if I had been shooting up each day and now missed my daily fix. I had to be with her again. I had to.

The next day I called Bernie Brillstein and told him to tell Gilda, "The ducks are quacking in the pond."

When Gilda arrived in Los Angeles with her suitcases, I met her at the airport and brought her home. I roasted a chicken for her that night, naturally. The next morning I made her some toast, which she always craved for breakfast, while I had a toasted raisin bran muffin. I made my usual Twinings Earl Grey Tea, and just as I started to read the front page of the New York Times, Gilda said, "Are you always going to eat that way?"

". . . What do you mean? What way?"

"Make noises that way, when you're chewing. Dibby says that you should keep your mouth closed when you're chewing, so that you don't make noises."

"Who's Dibby?"

"The lady who took care of me when I was growing up. Dibby always said it's impolite to make noises when you eat."

"But this is how I eat a bran muffin, Gilda. I mean—I don't want to worry about how open or closed my lips are when I'm eating a bran muffin. I don't think I was making much noise."

"Well, Dibby wouldn't like it."

I started to flush red, inside, but then "Margie" took over. I looked at Gilda's pretty face and realized that she was probably so afraid of my seeing *her* faults that she decided to strike first, choosing an area where *I* was at fault. I made some joke and said I would try to make Dibby happy. The next day—and all the days after—she never mentioned my chewing noises again.

One day, she decided to tell me what the horrible thing was that she couldn't tell me before. She was bulimic. I didn't know what the word meant. She explained it to me, in detail, and then said, "Don't ever monitor me. I'm working on conquering it by myself. But if you hear things or smell things, don't try to monitor me." It reminded me of when Katie was stuffing candy wrappers in her desk drawer and Margie said, "Don't talk to her about food."

I smelled something strange after dinner the next day and thought at first that some food had gone rotten and was sitting in the garbage pail. Then I heard the faucets being turned on in Gilda's bathroom, and then a little gargle. Then she came out of her bathroom, looking clean—as she always did—and smelling sweet. Not a trace of vomit when she kissed me.

It always happened after dinner, never after lunch or breakfast. She ate so sparingly and sensibly at those times. But after dinner, when she had indulged her cravings for food, she had to get rid of it quickly so that she wouldn't get fat. If I were reading in the living room, I could hear her vomiting in the bathroom, but I knew that I had to keep my mouth shut and pretend that I didn't hear or smell anything, as much it went against my natural instinct to try and help. In a restaurant she would excuse herself shortly after eating her main course and go to the ladies' room. She was always back in no time, cheerful as ever. She was losing her teeth, slowly, because of the acid in her vomit. When she did get professional help, specifically for the bulimia, she would talk to me about all these things. But that was months away, as was her divorce.

Now Gilda started a campaign to get us married. The psychiatrist she was seeing in Los Angeles told her to leave it alone or she might drive me away. I told Gilda that we weren't ready for marriage; that my reason for not wanting to get married, yet, was not about love, but about her dependency. I could hardly make a move without her wondering where I was, where I would be, why didn't I want to do this instead of that.

We went to her house in Connecticut for a short vacation. One afternoon, when I hadn't seen her for a few hours, I began searching the house—inside and outside—calling out her name. I called, "Gilda"—softly at first, and then I got worried and started hollering her name. No answer. I went up to her pink dressing room on the third floor . . . nothing. Then I went to every other room in her beautiful 1734 colonial house, then to the basement, then back up to her third-floor dressing room. I looked at the closet doors where she kept her dresses. The doors were closed, but some instinct led me to open one of them . . . and there she was, lying on the floor, in the dark. I knelt down beside her.

"What is it, honey? Please tell me. What are you doing in here?"

"I want to go home."

"You *are* home, Gilda."

I kissed her on her forehead, in the way that I assumed her

Dibby used to kiss her when she was a little girl, then held her for a little while and rocked her. Then she got up. Fifteen minutes later she was bouncing around the kitchen, singing a song, talking about what we should have for dinner—without even a mention of the closet.

I wouldn't say she was romantic—"How'd you like to just stick your thing in here right now?"—but she was *a* romantic in the sense that she always looked for a pair of rose-colored glasses to help her tolerate life. When she gave advice to other people, she was brilliant, and a realist, but she couldn't do the same for herself. I began to resent how much energy she poured into her fears and childish needs. She had to be first to order food (understandably, considering the bulimia); first to be served; first to say what *she* wanted, about anything, in any place. She was a little girl who needed attention, all of the time. We didn't get along well, and that's a fact. We just loved each other, and that's a fact. After living together for a year, listening to her talk about marriage day and night—I left Gilda.

I flew back to Los Angeles to continue writing. Gilda rented an apartment in New York, on the East Side, and asked her cousin Duane—who lived in Detroit and used to raise Yorkshire terriers—to please pick her out a good one and find someone who would bring it to New York; she would pay anything. A few days later Duane called her to say that he'd found a beauty—a little curly-haired female Yorkie named Sparkle. He had also found a young college student who was going back to NYU and who said she would be happy to take Sparkle on the plane with her, no fee, just as long as Gilda sent a car to pick them up at the airport.

After three weeks without her I was having a difficult time. I decided to fly to New York to see Margie . . . and perhaps Gilda.

It was nice to see Margie again—like seeing an old friend after many years. When I told her my situation with Gilda, she said, "You do what you have to do, but you should know that it's as difficult to conquer bulimia as it is to kick a drug addiction."

I went to the Carlyle Hotel that night and got my old room back, on the nineteenth floor, where Gilda had thrown me down on the bed and said, "I have a plan for fun!"

Gilda and I had a nice talk on the phone. She was in her apartment in Manhattan but was going back to her house in Connecticut the next evening, after her dog arrived. She sounded calm and very healthy. When she heard that I was staying at the Carlyle Hotel, she said that she'd meet me there the next evening, just for a short while before leaving for Connecticut, and that she would arrange for the college student to bring Sparkle to the lobby of the Carlyle.

When Gilda arrived, I thought she looked radiant. She was calm, cheerful, sensitive. We talked for half an hour and then Reception called to say that there was a limousine downstairs. We both went down. The young lady who had brought Sparkle from Detroit handed her over to Gilda. Sparkle seemed very content to be hugged and kissed by this new person. Gilda instructed the limousine driver to take the young lady home and then come back to pick her up for the trip to Connecticut.

When we got back to my room, Gilda gave the dog a bowl of water and set some newspaper down in the bathroom for her to pee on. After that was taken care of, I ordered the cheesecake and coffee that Gilda said she had a yen for, and then we continued talking. Sparkle didn't make a sound—no barking or whining or heavy breathing—she just sat on the floor and looked at the two of us. It must have been strange for her. She was a year old and had been taken from a farm by a stranger, put on an airplane, driven in a limousine, and then hugged and kissed by another stranger. Even when the doorbell rang, she didn't bark. I thought perhaps she wasn't able to bark. The waiter brought in the cheesecake and poured out some coffee for us. When Gilda and I started eating the cheesecake, we heard a little peep from Sparkle. She sounded more like a bird than a dog—a very polite bird—but it was obvious that she wanted her share of cheesecake, which Gilda gave her. So the three of us polished off the cheesecake—"One piece, three forks, please."

When we finished our dessert, I took Gilda down to the lobby and escorted her and Sparkle into the waiting limousine. We had a short kiss, and then I closed the door. We waved good-bye through the car window, and they drove off. Seeing Gilda looking strong and healthy and so happy with her little dog, I thought, *Maybe things between us can work.*

When I returned to Los Angeles, I went to see Gilda's psychiatrist, whom she used to see once a week. I wanted to talk to him about Gilda and marriage and my fears about living with her for the rest of my life, even though I loved her. He was kind and very understanding, but I sensed him pushing me gently towards marrying Gilda. I think he just wanted her to be happy.

During the fifty minutes I spent with him, the word "neurotic" came up a few times, and I asked him what that word meant to him. He said, "Trying to correct a wrong." I saw him again a week later, and we talked about Gilda a little more. Towards the end of that meeting, I said, "By the way, I like your definition of neurotic very much, but I would add one thing to it." "What's that?" he asked. I said, "Spending *too much time* trying to correct a wrong." He said, "I would accept that."

* * *

My daughter attended the University of Arizona for part of a year, until she got into a terrible accident. Before the accident, I met the young man she was attached to. I assumed they were living together, and my most generous opinion of him was that he was a dumb punk. I said to myself, *Be tolerant. They're just kids—*

she'll grow out of this stage. A few months later she rode up a steep hill, sitting on the back end of the punk's motorcycle. They were sideswiped by a big Buick, and Katie's knee was smashed.

Gilda had a close friend who was a doctor at Toronto General Hospital, in Canada. When she told him what happened to Katie, he recommended a great knee specialist in Toronto. I passed the information on to Jo, who made an appointment with the specialist and then took Katie to Toronto.

Gilda wanted me to meet Dibby—of noisy bran muffin chewing fame—who lived about an hour outside of Toronto. I met Dibby and thought she was wonderful. The next day Gilda and I went to visit Katie in the hospital. I was a little taken aback at the glow in Katie's eyes when she saw Roseanne Roseannadanna walk into her hospital room. I had only seen Gilda a few times on *Saturday Night Live,* but Katie had probably watched her every week. Gilda jabbered away and made Katie laugh, and then she gave Katie a pair of grotesque black-and-pink panties that she'd picked out in a porno shop.

The operation on Katie's knee was technically successful, but Katie had to walk with a cane for a long time after. That terrible accident changed her life in many good ways. She moved back to New York, got a job at *Good Morning America,* enrolled at Hunter College . . . and never wanted to see the dumb punk again.

THE DOG WHO TRIED TO COMMIT SUICIDE

You may have heard that Gilda and I were married by a dog. That's just silly. How could a dog possibly marry us? Sparkle didn't even have a license. It was probably just a rumor that Cousin Buddy was spreading around, although what actually happened is not really that much different.

We were living in Los Angeles, having just finished filming *The Woman in Red*. Gilda and Sparkle and I got ready for a grand vacation in the South of France. It was also going to be my birthday celebration. Then I received a call informing me that my sister had just found out she had breast cancer. Corinne lived in New York with her family. Gilda and I decided to take an early-morning flight to New York, see Corinne, and then fly to France the following day.

We got to Los Angeles airport early, and because we had Sparkle with us, the airline kindly put us in a private passenger lounge to wait for our flight to New York. We had the whole lounge to ourselves. Gilda took Sparkle out of her carrier case and set her on the floor, so she could bounce around and check things out before being cooped up on the plane. Gilda saw Sparkle sniff at something in a corner. When she went over and knelt down, she saw little blue pellets that had spilled out of a box that had RAT POISON clearly printed on the front. I said, trying to sound like a vet, "Now stop worrying! Sparkle would never eat that stuff. She's so finicky about everything she eats—why on earth would she want to eat some blue shit that she sees lying on a dirty floor?" The travel agent who was with us called the poison center and gave them the number on the box and the name of the poison. "Get her to a vet immediately," said the voice on the other end. Gilda grabbed Sparkle and said, "I'm going to the vet. I'll meet you in New York later." She kissed me good-bye and ran off with the travel agent. Gilda jumped into a limo that had just dropped someone off, and she screamed at the driver, "Take us to the nearest vet!"

In the meantime, my plane went out on the runway, had mechanical difficulty, and had to come back. Someone from the travel agency handed me a telephone number where I could call Gilda. When I reached her, she said, "The vet just gave Sparkle an injection that caused her to throw up a blue pellet. She did eat rat poison! She's shaking and scared and has to go on a program of vitamin K for two weeks. I have to take her back to the vet every day for the injections."

Well, so much for the straight line. Now here's the punch line. Before hanging up—after her sobbing and my apologizing for being so stupid—Gilda said, "Go see Corinne and then go to France. You're so tired, and you need a rest. I know you love me. You know I love you. I'll be fine. There's a little birthday present for you in the green suitcase. And don't worry about me—I'll be fine."

"Don't worry about me—I'll be fine." It may seem like small potatoes, but I had waited so long for her to say something like that.

I got to France, and on the morning of my birthday, I opened the green suitcase and found a small package wrapped in multicolored paper. Inside the package was a block of watercolor paper and a little palette with eight watercolor pots and two brushes, along with a note: "Happy Birthday, darling." That afternoon I painted my first watercolor. I've been painting watercolors ever since.

When I returned to Los Angeles, I proposed to Gilda. We were married on September 18, 1984. The irony is—and you have to believe me—if the dog hadn't eaten the rat poison, I honestly don't think that Gilda and I would ever have gotten married.

GILDA WANTS A BABY.

Gilda was making great progress with her bulimia—seeing a specialist who came to my home every week—and slowly, slowly, she was adjusting what she ate so that she wouldn't have to throw it up. She was thirty-eight years old.

Now she wanted a baby—"desperately," of course. I never had a strong desire to have children. Katie was enough for me, and I wasn't one of those men who felt that having your "own" baby was the important thing. But Gilda wanted a baby, and, as the song goes, "Whatever Lola wants, Lola gets."

After seeing her gynecologist, Gilda found out that her tubes were closed and that the only way she could ever have a child was by having a major operation, or by trying the in vitro fertilization procedure. I said that our relationship was more important than having a baby, but most of the decision was hers. I was against the major operation.

So every evening at six I gave Gilda hormone injections. I had learned how to give injections when I was in the medical corps, but I thought I'd better practice on a few oranges and grapefruits—the way I had been trained—before sticking needles into Gilda's buttocks. Actually, the skin of a grapefruit and the skin of buttocks are not that different, as far as toughness is concerned.

On the day that her ultrasound showed that she had matured enough eggs, I gave Gilda another injection to induce ovulation. The next morning I drove her to the hospital and watched the attendants wheel her into surgery to aspirate her eggs.

Then, as Gilda put it, *my* foreplay began. I was sent to the basement and put in a washroom, which had a scrub bucket, a mop, and five or six *Playboy* and *Penthouse* magazines to help me masturbate into a sterile plastic container. The pictures in the magazines almost put me off my job completely. I've always hated those color photographs of naked women in those stupid positions that are supposed to turn men on. I never felt that there was anything sexy about them. Alfred Hitchcock believed that what was really sexy was a woman in a long Victorian dress bending down to pick up a hanky and showing just a little bit of ankle and leg. I don't know about the long Victorian dress part, but otherwise I feel the same as Hitch.

For nineteen days after that I had to keep giving Gilda progesterone injections. On the twentieth day they gave her a blood test. It was negative. No baby. In February she booked herself for major surgery to have her tubes opened. She had the operation and recovered in a week. Her tubes were open, and she could now have a baby. All we had to do was have sex at just the right time of the month—exactly at the time she was ovulating.

Meanwhile, I had an idea for a film. I used to love watching *Creature Features* on television, with Katie and Jo, when Katie was afraid to watch those old horror films by herself. We all laughed at the scary parts. When I was a kid, I loved comedy/mysteries—especially Bob Hope in *The Cat and the Canary* and *Ghost Breakers*. The movie idea I had was to make my own comedy/horror film, but using the same techniques for visual effects that they used in the 1930s—where every visual effect was done *in the camera*, not at some visual effects plant, which cost a fortune and would ruin the concept.

One evening, Dom DeLuise came to my house for dinner and did his imitation of Ethel Barrymore, which made me laugh so much—because it was funny, of course, but also because it was so accurate. I asked Dom if he would play my aunt, doing his Ethel Barrymore, if I ever made a 1930s comedy/horror film. He said he would. The title I gave to the idea was *Haunted Honeymoon.*

Terry Marsh had recently written a film with Ronny Graham, and I wanted him to write *Haunted Honeymoon* with me, not only because I loved his humor but also because so much depended on what could and could not be done visually—an area in which he was an expert and I was almost ignorant. Orion Pictures said that they would give it a "go" *if* we did the film in England, because of the weakness of the English pound at the time.

Gilda dwelled on the fact that if I traveled without her, she would miss an ovulation cycle. She swore that I was the only person she ever slept with to get a part in a movie, and even though she wasn't right for the part in *Haunted Honeymoon*—whatever Lola wants she usually gets. Besides, Paulette Goddard was too old for the part.

Gilda did get pregnant while we were in England—for a week—and then had a miscarriage. But now she knew that she *could* get pregnant, and that made her happy. We finished filming in November of 1985 and came back to Los Angeles in time for Christmas. On January 6 she had her first symptom of ovarian cancer.

Gilda went to more internists, gynecologists, holistic doctors, and gastroenterologists than Carter has Little Liver Pills. She always asked the same questions: "Is it cancer?" The answer from all of them was the same: "No, no no . . . she just a highly strung woman." "She has Epstein-Barr virus." "Not serious—it's just *mittelschmerz*." "She's a very nervous girl" "Depression, stress, anxiety."

After ten months of no diagnoses or incorrect diagnoses—with her tummy distended as if she were hiding a small balloon under her dress—she finally heard it: "You have stage four ovarian cancer."

Gilda grabbed my face in her hands and sobbed, "No more bad news, no more bad news. I don't want any more bad news."

chapter 26

I DON'T BELIEVE IN FATE.

While Gilda was receiving chemotherapy, I received a script called *See No Evil, Hear No Evil.* Wonderful concept—terrible script. I turned it down.

Six months later, when Gilda was almost finished with her nine sessions of chemo, my agent sent me *See No Evil, Hear No Evil* again. "Are you crazy?" I asked. "I turned this script down six months ago."

A few months later, my *new* agent, Marty Baum, called: "I want you to meet the people at Tri Star about a script called *See No Evil, Hear No Evil.*"

I started to laugh. "Marty, I've turned this script down twice already. It's a great idea for a film, but it's a rotten script."

"I don't care—I want you to meet the people at Tri Star."

I went to Tri Star and told them exactly what I thought, including the fact that the script was pissing on the blind and the deaf, because whoever wrote it didn't know anything about either. They said, "We agree with you. We thought you might like to write it for yourself and Richard Pryor."

I told Tri Star that I would write twenty pages—starting over, but using the same concept. If they didn't like what I wrote, we would part friends and they wouldn't owe me a penny. If they did like what I wrote, I'd continue writing. Everyone agreed. Arthur Hiller was hired to direct.

* * *

Between her chemotherapy treatments, in the hospital in California, Gilda would come home and try to lead as normal a life as possible, but the first few days were always exhausting because she was so hyped up from steroids. Sparkle would spend day and night lying in bed at Gilda's feet, except when she was let out in the backyard to relieve herself. Occasionally she would whimper for Gilda to play with her, and if Gilda didn't respond, Sparkle would continue whimpering, until, going crazy from the steroids and rage at her condition, Gilda would sit up and pound the bed with her fists—as if she were pounding the cancer—and scream at Sparkle, "STOP IT! STOP IT!" At those times the little dog couldn't understand what was happening and she'd run to me to hold her. Gilda couldn't understand it either. I often felt the way that I imagined Sparkle felt—wanting to touch her, to smell her, and know that she was there, alive, and that she still loved us. Every once in awhile, when she was ready to go to sleep, she would pull the covers up around her head, like a little girl, and look at me with those huge brown eyes, and plead—as if I were her father—"Help me. . . . Please help me. . . . I don't know what to do."

I rarely got angry with Gilda, but when the kettle started to boil, I had to let some steam out, or I would have burst. At those times

I was the one who was pleading with her for help: "Gilda, for God's sake, try to think about something besides yourself. You're *not* a baby! You pretend to be—when you go to bed at night and you're frightened and I ask what's the matter and you say, 'What if I forget to breathe when I fall asleep?'—but you're not a baby—you're a grown woman! Think about Sparkle, think about me, think about all of the friends you have who love you—*just get off of yourself!* I don't know how to help you anymore than I'm doing. You treat me like shit all day, no matter how hard I try to please you, and then at night you want me to make everything all right . . . but I can't! I want to, but I can't!"

The odd part is that when I did have such an outburst, it made her feel better. She'd kiss me and point her finger at me like a schoolteacher and say, "I know you. . . . You wouldn't get angry with me if you thought I was going to die. Thank you, darling."

Then, when I calmed down, I'd say, "Gilda, you treat every stranger in the world with respect, no matter how much pain you're in. All I want is for you to treat me the way you would a stranger."

"But you're my husband—don't you understand? You're the only one I *can* yell at."

I heard through my sister that Katie had been in a hospital in New York with a terrible case of endometriosis and had just had an operation. I was so engrossed with Gilda's illness that I let contact with Katie go by the wayside. When I called Jo, I was told that the operation had been a nightmare, but that Katie was at her own apartment now. I tried to call Katie several times, but no answer. I wrote to her, but she didn't respond. After a week I called again . . . still no answer. Then I wrote again, hoping that she might actually read my letter: "If I've done something that hurt you, just tell me what it was, honey, please. If you don't tell me what's wrong, I can't fix it." She never answered.

My nephew, Jordan—who was a few years younger than Katie but had always been close to her—let me know how serious my problem with Katie was. He said that the last time he saw her, she told him he would have to choose: "Either your uncle or me."

Jordan, who has always been like a son to me, told Katie that he couldn't make that kind of choice. He's never seen her or talked with her since. I called Jo and asked her if she knew why Katie wouldn't talk to me. Jo said, "You mean you don't know?" I said, "No, that's why I'm asking you." "Well, if you don't know, I can't tell you," she said. Within those few words, I thought, was the kernel of why I left Jo and Katie years before. The only clue to Katie's behavior is something she said to Jordan . . . that when she was ill, she wanted me to take care of her the way I was taking care of Gilda. That may or may not be true—I have no idea, but if it is I can understand it.

I went to see Margie to ask her opinion. She said that she thought Katie was so filled with anger at her biological father— whom she had never met and who had abandoned her—that the best way to get back at him was to get back at her "father."

How could such an unhappy thing have come about? My intuition tells me that if she ever did tell me what I had done, I might give her some simple explanation—about how ill Gilda was—or I might just apologize for hurting her and ask her to forgive me. But then she might lose her anger, and I think—for reasons she's probably not aware of—that she needs to hold on to her anger. I know that I may never see Katie again. I hope that the little girl I loved and adopted will be able to let go of that anger one day.

During this time, two messengers from Heaven were sent to Gilda and me. The first was a gastroenterologist named Edward Feldman, whom we met when he was brought in to oversee Gilda's first operation. He would come to my house in Los Angeles, two or three times a week, after a long day of work, just to look in on Gilda. Very often, on his day off, he would bring his wife, Jane, and we'd all talk about silly things that would make Gilda laugh. My friendship with Ed Feldman was to play an unexpected role in my life.

The second messenger was a cancer therapist named Joanna Bull, whom Gilda found through the Wellness Community, in nearby Santa Monica. Joanna came to the house each week and would talk with Gilda for an hour. Whatever they talked about was working. I could see that Gilda was starting to get control of her life, and also starting to enjoy life again. Still no sex for me—that went out months earlier—but I never wanted to burden Gilda with a request for relief, by hand or mouth, and Gilda never mentioned the subject. In the meantime, the major blood test that indicated tumor activity, called CA-125, was returning to normal.

The gynecological oncologist in charge of Gilda's case was a gentle man. Before each chemotherapy session he'd sit with us for an hour, in Gilda's hospital room, talking and joking, and especially listening. After Gilda finished her last chemotherapy, she was given her second-look operation, where the doctor took tissue samples to see if there were any cancer cells observable. Two tissue samples were tainted; the rest were pink and clear. I kept telling her that the news was wonderful . . . only two out of forty-one . . . and I believed it. Gilda felt wonderful, but her doctor said he wanted her to have some radiation now. "Belt and suspenders," he would say. So she had her entire abdomen radiated.

When she was finished with the radiation, we went back to her house in Connecticut, "cancer-free," she used to say . . . and so we thought. But after three weeks—when she went to a local oncologist for her routine blood test—she was told that her CA-125 had gone up, quite high. She had to start chemotherapy again. She thought that the oncologist who told her this had death in his eyes. She even referred to him as Dr. Death, and she wouldn't see him again.

When we were in France, the spring before we were married—staying at Chateau St. Martin—we played tennis with a New York oncologist and his wife. His name was Ezra Greenspan. Ezra was a kind man, and he always managed to make Gilda laugh. When she found out that she had to start chemo again, she asked me to call Dr. Greenspan.

We went to New York to see Ezra, and, after looking at her records and tissue samples, he gave her a spurt of new life in the form of hope.

"Dr. Death told me I had cancer in my liver."

"*On* your liver," Ezra said, "not *in* it."

"Do I have to have chemotherapy again?"

"Yes, but not what you had before—your body gets used that stuff. We've got to fool it—give it a different combination of chemo every time. AND GET THE HELL OFF OF THAT MACRO-BIOTIC DIET YOU'RE ON! . . . It's all right if you're healthy, but not if you're sick. We need to fatten you up. Eat hamburgers, pork, whatever—you need iron!"

During the car ride home Gilda was bubbling over in anticipation of eating a big, juicy hamburger again, which she did as soon as I returned from Giovanni's Country Market.

Ezra put us in touch with a soft-spoken and very good-humored oncologist in Connecticut, Dr. Boyd, who agreed to work under Dr. Greenspan's supervision. His office was close to where we lived, and he came to Gilda's house every week to administer the chemotherapy himself, in our kitchen, while we all jabbered away, made jokes, and sometimes even had a glass of wine, as the new combination of chemicals was being infused into Gilda's vein.

chapter 27

THIRD MOVEMENT

While Gilda was throwing up in our bedroom in Connecticut, I was writing a comedy in the room just below her. It sounds oxymoronic, but absurdity was a familiar guest now.

Gilda got her chemo every Monday or Tuesday and always had a portable toilet next to her bed. I would check on her every half hour or so, and Grace—the extraordinary lady who took care of the house—would always make sure that everything near Gilda was clean and smelled nice.

Before coming to Connecticut, I had done research at the Braille Institute in Los Angeles for *See No Evil, Hear No Evil.* The Braille Institute gave me confidence in writing Richard Pryor's character—but now that I was in Connecticut, I needed to know about people who were profoundly deaf, which was the case with the character I was to play.

My assistant in Los Angeles called the New York League for the Hard of Hearing. They wanted to see a copy of what I had written thus far and said that I should call a certain Ms. Webb, who worked at the league as clinical supervisor.

Ms. Webb? Oh, my God! I thought *I'm going to get some cranky New England biddy out of* Our Town, *who's going to ask me, in her arrogant, raspy voice, "What are you trying to do—make fun of the deaf?*

With my heart beating a little faster than normal, I called the league and asked to speak to Ms. Webb. After a few moments a soft voice came on the phone.

"Hello—I'm Karen Webb."

"Oh! Hi, I'm Gene Wilder."

"Yes, I know."

"Did you get the script?"

"Yes I did. I think it's very funny."

"Oh, good. It's just a first draft."

"Well, I can see that it could do a lot of good for the hearing-impaired—especially with all the people who will want to see the movie if you and Richard Pryor are doing it."

"Thank you."

"But it's filled with inaccuracies."

". . . Yes. Well, I mean, yes—that's why I called *you*."

I was a little taken aback by how nice she sounded and also because she thought the script was funny. I made an appointment to come to the league the following week.

When I arrived, I told the receptionist that I had an appointment with Ms. Webb. After a minute, out came this lovely woman—in a lavender-and-pink dress—with a little touch of blue mixed in—that flared out just below her knees as she walked towards me. I hadn't had any sexual activity in so long that I tried, for

Gilda's sake, and mine, to suppress those natural urgings. But seeing Ms. Webb's dress sway back and forth brought an ache to my heart, not to mention my loins. She took me to her office and asked me to sit in front of a monitor.

"I'm going to show you a video of a woman talking. You won't hear any sound—I just want you to tell me what you think she's saying."

She started the video. I did my best to concentrate, until I realized that the pretty woman who was doing the silent talking was the woman in front of me . . . Ms. *Webb*. When the short video was over, I told her what I thought the woman was saying.

"Let's try it again," she said. "This time the camera will be closer."

She started the video. Now the camera showed her face just from her eyebrows to her chin. I concentrated again on what I thought she was saying, and I thought I did pretty well.

"Let's try it again," she said. "This time the camera will be closer."

She started the video again. Now it was a giant close-up of just her lips. I wanted to say, "Okay, I give." But of course—being the gentleman I am—I pretended to be studying her lips as if I were a scientist and tried to shut out any erotic thoughts. After a while I really thought that I did understand what those lips were saying.

"How'd I do? Pretty good, I'll bet."

"Fair."

After swallowing my pride with a silly joke, I told Karen that in certain scenes I would actually prefer *not* to hear what the other actors were saying. She sent me to the audiologist in the office next to hers, to have my ears fitted with skin-colored plugs that I could wear during the filming.

During the following two weeks, Karen sent me to Beginning, Intermediate, and Advanced lipreading classes (they call it "speech reading") where I could ask the clients any questions, about anything. I asked one group, "How do you feel when you read some cab driver's lips who's screaming at you, 'WHAT'RE YOU—FUCKING DEAF?' because you didn't stop when he honked his fucking horn—which you couldn't hear?" They all laughed, mostly because they had all been in that situation.

A bizarre concern cropped up two weeks before filming was to begin. A faction of the deaf community wanted Tri Star to hire "actually blind" and "actually deaf" actors to play the parts that Richard and I were going to play. I met with one representative and tried to explain that—even if they got what they wanted—what good would it do if no one went to see the movie? How funny could the actors be, compared to how many millions of people would pay to see Richard and me being funny? To give our film some moral ammunition, Tri Star and our director, Arthur Hiller, hired Karen Webb as technical consultant—with screen credit, but without pay.

See No Evil, Hear No Evil began filming in August. Gilda surprised me—and everyone else—by showing up at Union Square on our first day of filming. She had been driven from Connecticut and stayed to watch us for half an hour. She looked so pretty, wearing a skirt and blouse again, and a little makeup. I hadn't seen her in anything but one of her short nightgowns for so many weeks. Arthur Hiller cried, and Richard and I did our best to make her laugh. She was our audience. And she did laugh.

Of all the pleasurable times that Richard and I had on previous films—and there were some wonderful times, despite the difficulties—the experience on *See No Evil* was the happiest. Richard was sane and clearheaded and filled with good humor. A short while later he had a heart attack, and a short while after that he felt the onset of his multiple sclerosis.

* * *

Gilda developed a bowel obstruction. The radiation that she had had over her entire abdomen sought its revenge. All of her intestines reacted to any food passing through them in the same way that a severely sunburned person reacts to even the slightest touch of someone's hand.

On October 3 she had an operation to repair the blockage. She spent the better part of two weeks at Mount Sinai Hospital, with one of those nasogastric tubes in her nose. She hated it, like everyone does, but she couldn't have it removed until there were signs that her bowel was working, and the proof the doctors needed that the bowel was working was an unmistakable fart. After ten days she let fly with a small, but beautiful, fart. I was staying at the Carlyle Hotel during this time, and each evening after filming I'd go to the hospital and report all the funny things that happened during the day with Richard and me.

The doctors were able to repair Gilda's bowel obstruction. Biopsies revealed no tumor activity. Dr. Greenspan's program was working; she was able to eat again. I took Gilda back to Connecticut on my day off, and she and Sparkle had a grand reunion.

WITH EVERY GOOD-BYE YOU LEARN.

During the last week of filming *See No Evil, Hear No Evil,* Karen Webb invited me to her apartment for dinner. I don't know why I hesitated. I think it was because I was attracted to her and didn't want to cause problems. Then I decided that I was just being silly, and that I ought to accept her invitation, since I was so grateful to her for how much she helped us during the filming.

I walked into her apartment on East Ninety-eighth Street, and, after the usual hellos and small talk, I went into her kitchen to keep her company while she finished cooking dinner.

Browsing around as we talked, I saw that she had a long, pointed tea strainer, like the one I always used, except that hers was made of bamboo and mine was made of wire mesh. Resting next to her strainer was a can of Twinings Earl Grey Loose-Leaf Tea. I remarked on the coincidence of her choice of tea and method of brewing it. As I continued babbling, I noticed a bunch of notes and several small photos on one of her cupboards. There was a particular piece of paper, in a frame, that caught my eye. It had several lines printed on it. This is what it said:

"AFTER A WHILE"
Veronica A. Shoffstall

After a while you learn
the subtle difference between
holding a hand and chaining a soul

and you learn that
love doesn't mean leaning
and company doesn't always mean security.

And you begin to learn
that kisses aren't contracts
and presents aren't promises

and you begin to accept your defeats
with your head up and your eyes ahead
with the grace of a woman, not the grief of a child

and you learn
to build all your roads on today
because tomorrow's ground is too uncertain for plans
and futures have a way of falling down in mid-flight.

After a while you learn that even sunshine burns
if you get too much.

So you plant your own garden
and decorate your own soul
instead of waiting for someone to bring you flowers.

And you learn that you really can endure,
that you really are strong
and you really do have worth.

and you learn
and you learn
with every good-bye you learn.

After I read that framed paper, I stood in Karen's kitchen, watching her for the longest while. I didn't speak until she asked me something about roasted garlic, while she was pulling things out of the oven, and then she said, "We can sit down now—dinner's ready."

Dinner was delicious—lamb and roasted garlic, with lots of vegetables. She served a wine that I knew was expensive—too expensive for what I imagined her salary must be. I didn't want her to think I didn't appreciate the wine, but I scolded her, very gently, for spending so much money.

During dinner she told me that she was trying to get a grant to make a video that could be sent to libraries all around the country. It was going to be for people who couldn't come to New York but who were losing their hearing and wanted to learn how to read lips. Karen asked if I would help make it funny—keep it from being plain and dry—*if* she ever got the grant. I said I'd be happy to help. I had to leave fairly early that night since I had an early-morning call, so I told her I'd better be going. I held her hand on the way to the door and thanked her for the delicious dinner and for all the help she had given to the film.

When we arrived at the door, I didn't want to leave. I just stood looking at her—the memory of the poem on her cupboard was fusing with the face in front of me, and I longed to hold that face in my hands, just for a few moments, and kiss her. It had been such a long time since Gilda and I had kissed, romantically. I stopped thinking. I took Karen's face in my hands and kissed her. The way she responded seemed to be part passion and part compassion and, I think, part hope that we might meet again.

*   *   *

In November, Gilda, Sparkle, and I flew back to Los Angeles. Gilda had been working on a book for over six months and now Simon & Schuster was going to publish it. It was called *It's Always Something*. Originally it was going to be the story of a young comedienne from Detroit who becomes very famous, gets cancer, fights it with all her might and, miraculously, gets well. She had the ending in mind before she knew what the ending would be. Gilda had another operation at the beginning of 1989 to alleviate her burnt intestines. She felt better for awhile, but then her cancer went on a rampage. Six weeks before she died, she wanted to take singing lessons. She hired a singing teacher, who came to the house once a week. While he accompanied her on the piano, Gilda sang "When You Wish upon A Star."

Three weeks before she died, she pulled herself out of bed, put on a skirt and blouse, and was driven to a recording studio, where she made the audio copy of *It's Always Something*. She was forty-three years old when she died, on May 20, 1989. I buried her in a nondenominational cemetery three miles from her 1734 colonial home, in front of a tall white ash tree.

I used to go the cemetery several times a week, to say a few words to Gilda and to let Sparkle pee on top of her grave. I knew Gilda would love that. I don't go to the cemetery for *her* sake anymore—as if she might know each time I came and would be hurt if I skipped a week. I know she's not there. If I go now, it's for *my* sake. I used to worry all my early life about being good enough to please God. Gilda didn't think much about those things—she was just naturally good. I don't want to be a better person than Gilda— she was just human, and that's all I want to be . . . just human.

Before I met Gilda, I knew nothing about cancer. I was not only ignorant—I was dumb. Like many families, mine never mentioned the C word, as if by talking about cancer you could catch it. After Gilda died, one question kept intruding into my thoughts: if the blood marker they call CA-125 was used to detect tumor activity with women who had ovarian cancer, why couldn't they use it as a screening test for women who had symptoms like Gilda's, to *find out* if they had ovarian cancer?

I wrote to Gilda's New York gynecologist and asked her if she had ever thought to give Gilda a CA-125.

Dear Mr. Wilder:

Gilda was a wonderful woman with a great spirit. We'll all miss her. CA-125 is a blood test used after a diagnosis of ovarian cancer.

I talked with the coinventors of CA-125—Dr. Robert Knapp and Dr. Robert Bast. Both said that they were trying to change the conventional wisdom, so that gynecologists would use CA-125 to help determine whether or not a woman had ovarian cancer. Both men also cautioned that CA-125 wasn't foolproof—there could be false positives and false negatives—but it was the best available test until new ones were perfected.

Ezra Greenspan, the oncologist who gave Gilda hamburgers and a burst of hope to live on, for a while, said that if she had had a CA-125 when she felt her first symptoms, they would have found out that she was in stage three instead of stage four ovarian cancer, which would have given her a 20–25 percent better chance of survival.

With the help of my friend Bob Marty, who had his own video studio in downtown Manhattan, I made a Public Service Announcement that was directed to women over thirty-five, who had a family history of ovarian cancer. It was broadcast on all three major networks in the United States and reached ninety-three million women. Today, there isn't a gynecologist in America who doesn't know about CA-125 and its antecedents.

Of course, if any of the famous actresses had accepted the woman's part in *Hanky Panky* before Sidney Poitier finally offered it to Gilda, I would never have met Sparkle, who wouldn't have eaten the rat poison, which would have meant that Gilda and I wouldn't have gotten married . . . and all of the Gilda's Clubs in the United States, Canada, and England wouldn't exist.

chapter 28

COMEDIENNE—BALLERINA 1946–1989

I didn't know that Gilda was going to leave her beautiful 1734 home to me. It sounds stupid, but we never talked about such things. I also never believed that she was going to die of cancer—not until three weeks before she did die. I was a fool, and I'm grateful for that. My sublime ignorance gave her hope for a long while, and I know now that hope is the thing that keeps us going—allows us to laugh even in the worst of times.

After Gilda died, I thought that if I went back to Los Angeles, I would never return to Connecticut. So I wandered through the bedrooms and staircases and closets of Gilda's colonial house, late at night, in the dark, hoping to get rid of any ghosts that might be lurking in the corners. I yelled out loud to Gilda, on the off chance that she wasn't too absorbed with herself to listen. After a few weeks, roots started to grow, and I realized that I didn't want to live anywhere else for the rest of my life.

THE DRESS THAT CHANGED MY LIFE

In September of 1989 I got a call from the receptionist at the New York League for the Hard of Hearing, saying that a Ms. Webb wanted to speak to me. "Please put her on," I said.

While I was waiting for Karen to come to the phone, the image of the dress she wore on the day we met flashed through my mind—lavender and pink, with a touch of blue, swaying back and forth just below her knees as she walked towards me.

When Karen came to the phone, we talked about Gilda, and then she wanted to know how I was. I said I was doing well. "And how's little Sparkle?" she asked. I told her that although I had lost a wife, I gained a daughter—a tiny one—who wouldn't leave my side and who barks when strangers come to the door. Karen told me that she finally got the grant she was hoping for and that she wanted to know if I was still willing to help her make the video she had talked about. I said I'd be more than happy to help her.

Karen sent me the script she had written, with all the notes and statistics. Quoting Zero Mostel in *The Producers*, I told her, "This script will close on page four. Everyone will be asleep by then." We arranged to meet at my favorite Italian restaurant in Manhattan—favorite not just because the food was good, but because it only had eleven tables and was always quiet.

When we got to the restaurant, she set a tape recorder between us, on the table, and while we ate, Karen posed common problems for the hearing-impaired, such as trying to read the lips of someone who is chewing gum, or who has a bushy mustache, or who is standing in a shadow—and then I would improvise. She divided everything into short comedy sketches, which I thought was a brilliant idea.

The second time we met—at the same restaurant—we worked on improving the actual language that the characters in each sketch would use.

The third time we were going to meet, I asked her to leave the tape recorder at home. We had our first "actual" date on a beautiful fall evening, in the same restaurant, at the same corner table.

After we became lovers, Karen would drive to Stamford on most Fridays after work and stay with me for the weekend. She loved getting away from the city for a few days, and even though I lived on the edge of town, it was very much like being in the country: trees, deer, birds of all colors flying in and out of the bird feeders . . . and no tall buildings.

At dusk, when the deer came out to munch on the flowers in my backyard, Karen and I would watch Sparkle trying to chase the deer away from the rhododendron bushes. But the deer weren't at all intimidated by this little pipsqueak—they just kept eating the luscious white-and-lavender blossoms. Occasionally one of the deer would even try to play with Sparkle—or so it seemed—and Sparkle would look at us as if to say, "Aren't they supposed to run away?" Then she'd walk slowly back to us—obviously embarrassed—and the three of us would go in for dinner.

On those Indian summer evenings we ate on the screened-in porch at the back of the house. After dinner, when we were sipping our wine, I'd hold Karen's hand while we traded stories about our families and our childhoods. As I listened to her talk, my brain was split in two—part of me wanting to interrupt her to say, "I love you," and the other part warning me that once those magic words are spoken you can't go home again . . . not without pain.

When Karen asked me about Gilda, I told her funny stories, and a few sad ones. Karen told me about being on her own since her divorce sixteen years earlier, and about her father, Ira, who loved fly-fishing and liked his steak *very* rare, and her son, Kevin, who loved fly-fishing with his grandpa and liked his steak *very* rare, and her mother, Elsie, who never went fly-fishing—even though she loved to eat the fresh trout that her husband brought home—and who would never eat a steak if it wasn't cooked *well-done.*

As Karen talked, I kept flashing back to the first time she invited me to dinner in her apartment. Short phrases of the poem that she had tacked onto the cupboard in her kitchen kept popping into my head: ". . . the subtle difference between holding a hand and chaining a soul . . . you begin to understand that kisses aren't contracts." I thought, *Why would she put those beautiful thoughts on her cupboard door if they weren't part of her own philosophy?* But my brilliant rationale didn't stop me from hearing Gilda yelling in my ear, *"Hey! Don't you hurt this woman,"* or my heart from answering, *"Don't lose her. . . . Please, don't lose her!"*

LONG TIME NO SEE

March 1990

I walked into Margie Wallis's new office, on the first floor of her brownstone on the Lower West Side. She was sitting in her same comfy chair, but both of her legs were raised, resting on the ottoman. She told me on the phone that she'd had a hip replacement. I leaned over and gave her a little kiss.

ME: Long time no see.
MARGIE: I keep track of you, Gene.
ME: How are you doing, Margie?

MARGIE: I'm doing fine. Talk to me.

ME: I didn't think I'd ever get married again. I've been seeing a woman who isn't putting any pressure on me to get married—but I'm in love. Not just in love—I love who she is. Just saying, "I love you" isn't enough anymore—not for me. I want her to know that I love her so much that I want to spend the rest of my life with her, and I don't know how to say that in a better way than, "Will you marry me?"

MARGIE: But?

ME: If the tabloids start printing stories like, COULDN'T WAIT: GENE'S HOT NEW LOVE AFFAIR!—and they will—I'll feel terrible. I don't want to soil Gilda's name, and I don't want to soil Karen's name with that garbage. It's been almost a year since Gilda died, but everyone—on the street, in supermarkets, in cabs—still asks me about Gilda and my life with her. They keep saying, "Poor Gene—we love you both" I'm not poor Gene; I'm lucky Gene—to have found someone at this stage of my life.

MARGIE: Mister Sensitivity . . . did it ever occur to you that just because you ask a woman to marry you doesn't mean you have to get married the next day? If she knows and you know—you can tell Aunt Tillie and Uncle Harry and the rest of the world whenever you're ready to tell them.

ME: . . . I knew there was a reason why I came to you years ago—apart from your good looks and your total lack of sarcasm.

That night I stopped off at a tiny Russian restaurant, called Kalinika, on Eighty-second and Madison. It only had five or six tables, but if you called ahead, you could order most of their tasty dishes for takeout. I bought some cold beet borscht, Russian hors d'oeuvres, and a ginger chicken and took them to Karen's apartment.

When she answered the door, she was wearing a lavender caftan. I had told her that I was bringing dinner. After she closed the door, we had a lovely kiss, and then I said I wanted to talk to her for a minute before we ate. I think she was a little worried by the seriousness in my voice. I sat down on one of the three chairs in her small living room. She sat on my lap. I tried to breathe quietly for a moment and finally said, "Will you marry me?" Karen stared at me for the longest time, with a Mona Lisa smile that neither I nor Leonardo could have deciphered at that moment. Then she said, "You want to marry me?" I said, "I love you and want to be with you for the rest of my life." She broke into a full smile and said, "Yes . . . I will marry you," and hugged me.

On September 8, 1991, Karen and I were married in the backyard of the home in Connecticut that Gilda had left me. Seven people and a Yorkshire terrier were in attendance. Judge Gerald Fox—who had never performed a marriage service before—came to the house, wearing a heavy suit on this swelteringly hot, but beautiful day. He performed the short ceremony with sweat dripping off his happy face while his wife snapped pictures. Karen and I wrote, and spoke, the following:

UPON OUR MARRIAGE
We both believe in music and painting
and the truth that we can see all around us in nature.
We also believe that something, some fate,
brought us together at this exact point in both of our lives.
With appreciation for these exquisite insights,
and with the love and respect we both feel for each other,
we think we have the foundation for a happy life . . .
so long as we keep laughing.

I had turned down the script of *See No Evil, Hear No Evil* three times, and if my agent, Marty Baum, hadn't said, "I don't care what you think of the script, I want you to meet these people at Tri Star," I would never have met Ms. Webb at the League for the Hard of Hearing. And now I'm married to that cranky old New England biddy with the arrogant, raspy voice . . . but, boy, is she beautiful.

chapter 29

IT'S ALWAYS SOMETHING.

Gregor Samsa awoke one morning to discover that he had been transformed into a giant insect—in Kafka's short story, "Metamorphosis." In 1999 I awoke one morning to discover that I had a problem not so different from old Gregor's . . . a sharp pain on my left side that turned out to be non-Hodgkin's lymphoma. I don't like talking about cancer—and I don't intend to do much of it now—but there are a few ironies that can't be overlooked. It's not a sad story.

A very kind hematological oncologist whose office was only twenty minutes away, arranged for me to have nine chemotherapies, one every three weeks. I had my first chemo in the doctor's office while Karen read to me from *She's Come Undone* by Wally Lamb. I had supposed—because of my experiences with Gilda—

that I would be either extremely anxious or not anxious at all. I was not anxious; I don't know about the "at all" part—you'd have to ask Karen—but I was very calm and, to my great surprise, because of a wonderful new drug that Nurse Mary Harvey infused into my bloodstream while she dripped in the chemo, I didn't get sick or nauseous, not even for a minute.

After I did that first chemo, I went to New York in the afternoon to do publicity videos for *Murder in a Small Town*, a murder mystery that I had done for Arts and Entertainment a few months earlier. I told the crew to hurry up, because my hair was going to start falling out any minute. When my hair did fall out, after two-and-a-half weeks, my doctor kindly agreed to let Mary Harvey come over and give me the chemo in my living room. After two treatments my spleen had returned to normal size, and I was told that I wouldn't need nine treatments, just six.

During my third treatment, while I joked with Mary Harvey as she was dripping in the chemo, Karen handed me our portable phone. It was Mel Brooks.

MEL: How ya doing?
ME: Great.
MEL: When do you get your chemo?
ME: Now.
MEL: Whaddya mean?
ME: I'm getting it now, while we're talking.
MEL: Where?
ME: In my living room.
MEL: Well—how do you feel?
ME: Great.
MEL: When do they think you'll be able to eat again?
ME: In about fifteen minutes. We're having veal chops, linguini, a little salad, and some red wine.

MEL: How can that be?

ME: A new drug called Zofran. They didn't have it in time for Gilda.

MEL: It's a miracle. Which wine?

ME: Larose Trintadon.

After we hung up and I walked Nurse Harvey to her car, Karen and I sat down at the kitchen table and had our lovely meal.

When I finished my fifth chemo, my doctor said that he would give me one more and then something called rituxan for four weeks, and that would be it. All done! Apart from losing my hair, which I knew would come back, I felt fine—playing tennis with a pro, indoors, twice a week, and playing in a hard men's doubles game each Saturday.

I decided to call my dear friend Ed Feldman—the gastroenterologist in Los Angeles who had looked after Gilda so lovingly. I wanted to share the good news with him. When he heard the news, he said, "I'm very happy for you, Gene, but I'm not content . . . not until you see Carol Portlock at Sloan-Kettering."

I had my medical history and tissue samples sent to Dr. Portlock's office and made an appointment. Karen and I went to see her a few days later.

Carol Portlock was tall, very blond, and quite thin. She was cordial, but reserved. I was expecting some cheery news, but from the subtle hints in her face, I suddenly wasn't sure.

"You're very healthy," she said, "very chemo-responsive. But it's going to come back."

I was stunned. Karen's face froze.

"When?" I asked.

"In six months," she said, so assuredly that I didn't question it. After a long pause to catch my breath, I asked her what I could do.

"Stem-cell transplant."

I asked what that meant. She made an appointment for me to see Dr. Stephen D. Nimer, who was the head of hematological oncology at Sloan-Kettering.

Karen and I went to Dr. Nimer's office the next day. I took to him like a fish to water. Over two-and-a-half hours, he took us through every phase of what would happen to me and how I might feel—if I decided to have the stem-cell transplant. He pulled no punches. Every discomfort was described in detail by Nancy, the nurse practitioner who worked with Dr. Nimer. I was told that I would be in the hospital from four to six weeks, depending on how things went, but that I should count on six weeks. When Dr. Nimer was finished, he asked if I had any questions.

"When can I act again?"

"When do you want to act again?"

"In six months. I'm supposed to do another one of my murder mysteries in May."

He looked at me with such a beneficent smile and said, "You're a painter, aren't you?"

This shocked me. I didn't remember telling him anything about painting. I suppose I must have mentioned it in passing, but the question seemed like a non sequitur, given what we had been talking about.

"Yes . . . Karen and I paint watercolors."

"How would you feel if—just as you were about to finish a painting—someone came along and mucked it all up?"

I stared at him a long while. What was he getting at?

"You and I are going to paint a beautiful picture together. In six months you're going to feel pretty normal—but your immune system will only be about 80 percent of what it should be. Why don't you give it another two months? We don't want anyone to ruin our painting, do we?"

"SOLD!"

I went to Greenwich Hospital for an overnight stay on two occasions, two weeks apart, and they dripped in heavy chemo while I slept. No nausea. I would get up the next morning and go out and play or write or do anything I wanted. The heavy chemo encouraged the production of baby stem cells in my bloodstream. They weren't red or white cells yet—it was almost as if they wouldn't decide which color they wanted to be until they grew up. When my blood test shouted, "This guy is ready," I rushed to Sloan-Kettering, as an outpatient, and—while I was watching television— the doctor in charge extracted stem cells from my blood. It doesn't hurt; you don't feel anything. The machine takes your blood while you're reading or watching television, extracts the stem cells, and then sends the rest of your blood back into your body. The whole thing takes about an hour and a half. You go home, come back the next day, and do it again. After three days they had extracted seven million stem cells, which they put into a small plastic bag and froze.

That Christmas, before entering Memorial Sloan-Kettering for the long stay, I gave Karen a beautiful, but simple, necklace and wrote the following poem on a little card:

> *Of all the Mormons I've ever met,*
> *You're the first I ever et.*"

The day before I entered Sloan-Kettering, I was told that because I was in such good shape, they were going to knock the shit out of me with radiation and heavy chemo, and then pour the

stem cells back into my bloodstream. That night I had the following dream:

GENE'S DREAM

I was on the fifth floor of a dilapidated apartment house, where
I lived in a one-room artist's garret. Because of some great
emergency I had to leave my room, but it was suddenly invaded by a small herd of prehistoric bulls, with long antlers.
The bulls weren't threatening, they were just frightened, and
the only way to get them out of my room was for me to whistle
for a herd of black stallions to come upstairs, as quickly as they
could, and carry the frightened bulls down the four flights of
stairs and outside, to safety.

I went to the top of the stairs and whistled as loudly as I
could, and, to my great relief, a herd of black stallions came
rushing up the stairs and started rounding up the bulls—putting them on top of their backs and ushering them out.

But there was one bull, with long antlers and some human
features protruding through his animal hair, who was trying to
teach himself to play a violin that had been resting on a small
table in the center of the room. And although he wasn't playing
a melody as such, the sounds he was producing were beautiful.

I looked at him while he was playing, and I said to myself,
"How is this possible? This young prehistoric bull has just
picked up a violin and is not only figuring out how to play it,
but is playing beautifully."

Then I got terribly worried about how much time was passing and about the imminent danger—whatever it was. I
pleaded with the bull to put down the violin, but he kept saying, "Not yet . . . wait . . . a little more."

I finally got him to put the violin on the table just as a beautiful black stallion came up, and, together, we got this unique

bull onto the stallion's back and safely down the stairs. And then I woke up.

*   *   *

I checked into Memorial Sloan-Kettering on January 30, 2000, under the name of Larry Carter—which was my character's name in the murder mysteries. That evening, just after I had settled into my hospital room, the phone rang. Karen answered and heard, "Hi, this is the *Blah Blah County News*—how's Gene doing? We know he's there under the name Larry Carter—we were just wondering how he is." Karen said, "You have the wrong number." We changed rooms.

The next four days were not painful—I had radiation each morning and in the late afternoons—then they dripped in very heavy chemo for five days. Still no nausea. By now every cell in my bloodstream had been killed, and I didn't have an immune system to speak of. Anyone who came into my room—every doctor, nurse, cleaning lady—had to wash his or her hands, put on rubber gloves, and wear a mask. Karen was not allowed to use my bathroom—she might contaminate it. I made a joke and said, "Come on, she wouldn't do that," but she was told that if she needed to pee, she had to take off her gloves and mask, throw them away, walk down the hall to the ladies' room, come back to my room, wash her hands again, and put on a new mask and a new pair of gloves. Karen came to see me each day. When it was time to say good night, she would kiss me good-bye through her mask. In a strange way it was very romantic. I thought I was in a movie.

In the middle of all these treatments, the press representative for Sloan-Kettering came to see me—wearing her gloves and mask, of course—and told me a story out of Grimm's fairy tales, except that it had just happened in the lobby downstairs. A young woman walked into the lobby of the hospital, carrying a huge basket of flowers for Larry Carter. The chief of security recognized this woman's face and said, "What are you doing here?" The woman said, "Oh, shit—I can't do this. *STAR* sent me. They want me to get into Gene Wilder's room and get an interview. Here, give these flowers to anyone who wants them—this is too sleazy for me."

What *Star* didn't realize was that if the young lady had succeeded in getting to the floor I was on and had walked into any of the rooms with stem-cell patients while she was looking for me, she could have jeopardized their lives, because—I'm sure—she wouldn't have known to throw the basket of flowers away, wash her hands, and put on a pair of gloves and a mask before entering the room.

After four days of radiation and five days of the heavy chemo, they gave me a day of rest. On the eleventh day, Karen and I watched three technicians march into my room, wearing masks and gloves and carrying a tiny plastic bag with six million stem cells, all thawed out. (They had taken seven million, but they like to keep one million in reserve.) Everyone sang "Happy Birthday" while the stem cells were being infused into my bloodstream. They weren't singing because it was my actual birthday but because it was the first day of my new life—February 10, 2000. They had told Karen to bring a bag of lemons because, for some reason, when they pour in the thawed stem cells, there is a strong smell of garlic. I thought it was a joke, but it wasn't. I had to pass half a lemon back and forth under my nose while the infusion took place, or else the smell of garlic would have been overwhelming.

The next ten days were the most difficult except for one thing that I keep in a small treasure chest in my memory. Each evening, after he had finished his long day in the research lab and after attending to his other stem-cell patients, Dr. Nimer would come into my room, masked and gloved, pull up a chair, and talk with me about movies. He would answer any medical questions, of course, but afterward he loved to talk about movies. Because of his work he had missed so many good films over the years, but now most of them were on video or DVD, and he wanted to know which my personal favorites were and who was in them. When my throat was too sore for me to talk, I would write my answers on a long, yellow legal pad:

> ... City Lights, Random Harvest, Dark Victory, Bringing Up Baby, City for Conquest ...

He had never heard of most of them. The only thing missing from our evening soirées was a nice cold glass of Sancerre.

While Dr. Nimer sat with me each evening, those little stem cells were busy multiplying, deciding if they wanted to grow up to be red or white. After the ten days of misery were over, I started talking about going home.

On February 24—after only three weeks and four days in the hospital—I was told that I could go home with Karen that night, if my platelets had reached fifty thousand. If they hadn't reached that number, I might bleed to death if I happened to cut myself shaving.

The night nurse, Suzie, took some blood. An hour later she came back, trying not to look grim as she said, "Forty-eight thousand!" Karen took my hand and said, "It's only one more day, sweetheart." Then she leaned over and gave me a long good-night kiss, through her mask. It was the only time I cried during my stay in the hospital. Dr. Nimer had told me that same afternoon that I was getting out in record time and that I was now the poster boy, but I wanted to go home with Karen that night. I suppose I was crying because I came so close. After Karen left, I asked Suzie when they would take my blood again. She said, "Tomorrow morning, six-thirty. I'll take it myself."

While Suzie was loading my intravenous for the night, babbling quietly while she worked, I kept thinking about Karen and the way she kissed me good night through her mask. How could it have happened that I found her at this stage of my life? If we had met twenty years earlier, it wouldn't have worked. I know that. I wasn't ready for her, and she probably wasn't ready for me. Then I suddenly remembered a most curious incident.

Several years earlier, I was having supper with Karen's family in the little town of Arco, Idaho, population eleven hundred. There were eight of us at the kitchen table—seven Mormons and a Jew. One of the children—a four-and-a-half-year-old boy named Michael—had finished his supper of fresh trout and boiled potatoes and was looking at a child's astronomy book that he always carried with him. Michael's mother explained to the rest of us how much Michael loved astronomy.

"Go ahead," she said, "ask him a question. Anything!"

"All right," I said, taking up the gauntlet. I just wanted to see how this little pisher would deal with a real question.

"Michael," I said, "why does everything weigh less on Pluto than it does on Jupiter?"

I hadn't a clue what the answer was, and I hoped that I wasn't embarrassing him. Michael looked at me as if I were the dumbest person on earth. With an unbelieving 'Jack Benny' face, he looked at everyone else sitting around the table. Then he looked back at me, and with a shrug of his shoulders, he said, "Gravity."

Suzie interrupted my little memory with, "Do you want me to turn out the hallway light, sweetie?"

"Yes. Suzie, wait! I'll give you a million dollars if you do me a special favor."

"You're not ready for that yet."

"Hey—I'm trying to stay sad and you're not helping. All I want you to do is get a bunch of cotton and tape it over the speakers in this room so that I can't hear the P.A. system going on all night. I don't mind it during the day, but I can't stand it at ten or eleven o'clock when I'm trying to fall asleep and I suddenly get this blast over the loudspeaker: "JUANITA, JUANITA—REPORT TO THE DESK PLEASE. JUANITA, REPORT TO THE DESK." The nurses should wear those silent buzzers. This would be a wonderful hospital if it weren't for 'Juanita, Juanita.' "

Susie hesitated for a moment. "You won't tell anyone?"

"I promise you I won't tell."

Susie got a big pile of cotton and taped it over the two speakers in my room with adhesive tape. Then she took my temperature one last time and said, "Good night, sweetie—try to sleep."

And I did try. I thought that if I could just fall asleep, the sadness over not going home would dissolve into a dream, and then Suzie would wake me at six-thirty and say, "Get up sweetie—time to take your blood." But I couldn't fall asleep. The thoughts kept rushing in. *Maybe I'll be home tomorrow. Where can I buy some platelets, fast? Will I be able to act again in six months? I wonder if I'll be alive in six months. I want to kiss Karen without the mask. When will I be able to make love again? When will my hair grow back? And my eyelashes? I forgot about my eyelashes. I look pathetic. I wonder if Karen will still desire me when I get home. Actors are children. We're all just babies. "Look at me! Look what I can do!" Why didn't we grow up like other kids? All we wanted was to be loved for ourselves, just as we were, our true selves—but it didn't seem to be good enough, and when we're six or seven, and Mama is sitting in the living room crying or reading a book or sewing, and we tell a joke that we saw in a cartoon, or we do a little dance or sing a song, and suddenly Mama gets up and says, "Oh, my God—honey, that's wonderful. Bill, come in here—look what your baby can do! Do it again, honey—do that for Daddy." And we sing or dance or tell our joke again, and they applaud. Mama and Daddy applaud, and they hug and kiss us and we feel that they really love us, and we grow up longing for that exhilaration again, and we do* get it, years later, from an audience that applauds and cheers us and we go home exhilarated and fall asleep feeling loved, but the next morning we wake up feeling lonely again, and we need another fix from another audience. I wish I could be a Catcher, like Holden, and save all those lonely children who become actors and grow up thinking that the applause is actually love for them and not for their performance. Maybe some of them will find real love . . . if they're lucky.

"JUANITA, JUANITA—REPORT TO THE DESK PLEASE. JUANITA, REPORT TO THE DESK!"

Oh no! Come on, I can still hear it, Suzie. It's better, but I can still hear it. What time is it? . . . Ten o'clock! . . . Oh, no . . . miles to go before I wake. "Now I lay me down to sleep. . . . If I should die before I wake" . . . Well, so what if I do? I have no complaints. I had a wonderful career and beautiful friends . . . and I found Karen . . . gravity. . . . Oh, shit . . . I forgot something, Karen. . . . I was going to tell you something when you were kissing me good night. . . . I was going to whisper in your ear, "i carry your heart with me. . . . i carry it in my heart. . . ." How could I have forgotten? . . . because I was crying like a baby just because they wouldn't let me go home with you. . . . I wonder why e. e. cummings wrote poems in lowercase? . . . I'm getting drowsy. . . . Ativan must have kicked in. . . . Good . . . I can still feel you kissing me through your mask. . . . I won't ever forget that. . . . I'll tell you tomorrow how much I love you . . . but I gotta get some platelets. . . .

At 6:30 A.M. Suzie woke me up and took my blood. She came back at 7:30 A.M. with a big smile on her kisser: "Fifty thousand, you lucky duck!"

Now here's a question: did I actually will my body to produce two thousand platelets while I slept, or did Suzie slip me some kind of a verbal placebo, if there is such a thing—something tricky that she might have babbled while she was loading up my intravenous? What difference does it make? I'm going home! Suzie was right—I am a lucky duck. I keep thinking of the children I saw in the basement of Sloan-Kettering, five and six years old, bald from chemotherapy and sitting next to me in their wheelchairs, waiting to receive their radiation. The old urge to pray would cross my mind when I saw them, but I gave that up a long time ago. What is God, but something inside of me? What I wish for those children is just some good genes, and a very good doctor—that's what I wish for them.

If I escape death, it will be for one reason that I *can* believe in— it will be because of a phone call I made to my friend Ed Feldman to tell him how well I was doing. "All I need is one more chemo, Ed, then a little rituxan, and I'm all done. Isn't that something?" And Ed answered, "I'm very happy for you, Gene, but I'm not content . . . not until you see Carol Portlock at Memorial Sloan-Kettering."

* * *

chapter 30

STOLEN KISSES

It's a cold and sunny morning as we arrive back home. When we get out of the car, I have a strong urge to walk to the mailbox, just to see if I can do it, but I'm a little wobbly, so I'll try it tomorrow.

Karen lays on a beautiful fire in our big 1734 fireplace. She covers my body with a blanket that doesn't itch, and I take off my shoes and put my feet up on the old Spanish coffee table, which used to be a door about a hundred years ago.

I can't really swallow anything yet—I mean nothing that I would call food—but Karen thinks of a divine solution: vanilla milkshakes, with lots of vanilla ice cream. There's a wine in France called L'enfant Jesus, so named because the winery is run by a charity hospital in Beaune, and the story goes that when the nuns first tasted it they said, "It goes down like the little baby Jesus." On

this first day at home, I name her milkshake "Karen's divine milk."
It goes down my throat so cool and so easy.

For supper I have a mixture of Rice Krispies and Cheerios, with
lots of milk and a little sugar. Then we go up to our bedroom. I
look in the mirror as I brush my teeth and think I'm seeing someone who just got out of Auschwitz. When we go to bed, we watch
television for a few minutes. When I start to get drowsy, I kiss
Karen good night. I don't have to kiss her through a mask anymore. I'd like to do more than just kiss her, but I'm not ready for
that yet. Perhaps I'll try tomorrow, or next week, when I get some
strength back. Instead, after we've both said good night and turned
out the lights, I reach out and run my fingers over her bare arm
and fall asleep holding her hand . . . in my own bed.

When tomorrow comes, I walk up the driveway to the mailbox
and then back to the house. It's not that far—maybe a hundred
yards all together—but that's enough for one day. Tomorrow I'll go
back and forth two times. I tell Karen that I'm going to be playing
tennis with her by the last week in April.

On April 26 I play a very short game of tennis with her. On this
day she could beat me even if she played left-handed and hopped
on one leg. *But I don't fall over*—that's the important thing, although I almost did, twice. But I do get the ball back, most of the
time. In a few weeks I'll beat her so badly that she'll think I turned
into Agassi. Well, I don't want to humiliate her.

Six months later, and I'm still alive. My sister came through her
cancer and is doing really well. . . . We both must have good
genes. What I've learned from cancer is not about appreciating all
the little things in life that you take for granted. After Gilda died, I
was already that person who walked by a rose and noticed the
shades of red and orange and yellow and who could smell the rain
and could get a thrill at seeing two children holding hands. . . . I

know that stuff. What I didn't know was that I don't *need* to act. I might *want* to act—just for the love of acting—but not because I need to earn the right to feel loved by God. I've got something much better. . . . I feel loved by the person I love.

My blood tests are very good, and I've started painting again. Karen and I hit with a tennis pro twice a week. I think I'm getting a little chubby—not so much in the face, but around the middle. I even thought of dieting, but Mel warns me that men's faces look hollowed out if they get too thin when they're older.

I can make love with my wife again. And here's the amazing thing: it feels as exciting now as it did when we had our first actual date, when she was still a stranger to me.

EPILOGUE

Four and a half years have passed and I'm now in complete remission. I'm one of the lucky ones.

I paint watercolors again—I'm having a show at the New Britain Museum of American Artists—but I can't seem to paint when I'm acting or act when I'm writing or write when I'm painting. I don't know why. I'm sure it's the same energy, but that energy gets so possessive sometimes.

Karen and I also take tap dancing lessons once a week. It started out because I had written a musical for Whoopi Goldberg and me and I needed to dance in the film. Karen found a wonderful teacher named Gail Smith and even though the movie project fell apart Karen thought it would be good if we both kept on dancing.

There is one strange irony that I haven't told you. One April afternoon, three weeks before she died, Gilda walked up to me in our living room and said, "I have a title for you, 'Kiss Me Like a Stranger' . . . maybe you can use it some day." I had no idea why she said it or what the title meant; I just thanked her.

Fourteen years later I started writing this book. I had a completely different title in mind when I began; I was going to call it, "I Lean Towards Women." A terrible title, I think now: sounds like the story of a man whose right leg is shorter than his left. What I meant by it was only that I'm immediately comfortable with most women I meet, but with men it takes a little time.

As I was nearing the end of this book, recalling the tortures that Gilda had gone through and how she screamed and pounded on the bed, scaring the daylights out of Sparkle and me, I remembered how I had begged her to treat me at least with the kindness that she showed to every stranger she met. With Karen, because of some accidental beneficence, which I still don't understand, loving her each day feels almost the way it did when she and I first met. So the title Gilda gave me that April afternoon fourteen years ago took on a significance that I never would have imagined.

acknowledgments

To my sister, Corinne Pearlman, who always led the way.

To my editor, Elizabeth Beier, whose great power was in her gentle hints and suggestions.

To my friend, William Sarnoff, who steered me through uncharted waters.

index

Look for *The New York Times* bestselling author
Gene Wilder's elegant first novel,

My French Whore

in stores winter 2007.

St. Martin's Press
www.stmartins.com

38378167R00168

Made in the USA
San Bernardino, CA
04 September 2016